ANNA KOREN
THE SECRET SELF

translated by Edward Levin and Deborah Harell

A COMPREHENSIVE GUIDE TO
HANDWRITING
ANALYSIS

illustrated by Kobi Zaid

·K·U·P·E·R·A·R·D·

KUPERARD (LONDON) LTD
30 CLIFF ROAD, LONDON NW1 9AG

THE SECRET SELF
A Comprehensive Guide
To Handwriting Analysis
by Anna Koren

Copyright © 1987 by Anna Koren & Adama Books
This edition published by Kuperard, (London) Ltd., 1988

No part of this publication may be reproduced,
stored in a retrieval system, or transmitted
in any form or by any means, electronic, mechanical,
photocopying, recording, or otherwise (brief quotations
used in magazines or newspaper reviews excepted),
without the prior permission of the publisher.

ISBN 1-870668-03-0

Design: Yoav Graphica
Typesetting: M. Rachlin Ltd.
Production : Ruth Eilat
Printed in Israel

Introduction

I was interested in graphology even before I could read. Most of my early drawings were attempts to draw letters. Looking at letters other people wrote gave me a feeling of closeness to the writers, a feeling which I still have. I remember when I was about four years old I saw a blue envelope with red lines; I realized that it had come from far away, since its size and shape were different from the usual envelopes. The handwriting was somewhat shaky. When I brought it to my mother, I asked her what was wrong with the uncle who had written the letter. My mother asked me what I meant.

The answer was clear as day to me: "Can't you see for yourself? He's sick."

"What are you talking about?" But when she started reading the letter she turned pale, she learned that my uncle in Paris had undergone an operation, and had written the letter while convalescing.

This was the only topic at the dinner table that night. Everyone in the family looked at me as if I were a sorcerer or witch. No one thought of the possibility that I had seen the shakiness of my uncle's handwriting, and even I was not capable of verbalizing my intuition. To this very day, when people ask me during my lectures how I can see tension in someone's handwriting, my instinctive response is always, can't you see??

From the time I was a teenager until my daughters were born, I corresponded with many pen pals, practically with anyone who would agree to write to me. There were periods when I corresponded with dozens of people my age. I always experienced the strongest emotions during the first few minutes after opening the envelope, when I looked at the handwriting. The handwriting said more to me than the contents of the letters.

As time passed I learned that not everyone had the same feelings, not everyone could see what I saw in the script. I realized that I had to prove what I saw. I began to conduct research and started collecting samples of every person's handwriting that came my way, classifying and analyzing each sample.

Today, I can explain every characteristic revealed by handwriting. I have a collection of half a million handwriting samples and, believe me, I've learned a lot from them. I have taught hundreds of students in three-year courses (each of whom is accepted after an analysis of his or her handwriting). My best students have become graphologists in their own right, and have given courses to many more students.

This book does not tell the entire story of graphology. In fact, we are still in the pioneering stages of this science, a science which is being developed throughout the world. I hope that this modest volume will help you gain a better understanding of yourself and the world around you. This will be the true benefit of my research.

I want to thank the people who worked so hard to prepare this book: Tova and Devora, who worked for long months translating, typing, editing, retyping. Special thanks to Uri, Mazal, Rudi, and David, who collected professional literature throughout the world. And of course, thanks to my husband and daughters, for their patience, encouragement, and support.

Anna Koren
Haifa, Israel

Contents

What Is Graphology?

Many people talk about graphology, but few understand what this word really means. The literal meaning of graphology is "the science of writing." But what is "the science of writing"?

Functionally, writing is a basic means of communication among people. We would find it hard to imagine life without it. Physically, it consists of a system of lines, circles, semicircles, commas, points, and spaces – all more or less constant.

Graphology does not relate merely to the physical aspects of handwriting. It would be more accurate to describe graphology as the psychology of handwriting, defining the writer's personality and character. To learn more about it, we will examine the formal and rhythmical aspects of writing: the pattern and speed of movement; the difference between a child's printscript and adult handwriting; individual ways of composition; and the way a writer relates to a page.

Handwriting is actually the writing of the brain. As we know, the brain is responsible for the functioning of all voluntary and involuntary body mechanisms. It contains the centers of thought, feeling, and movement, and sends out reactions to various stimuli.

Handwriting is merely a product of the brain's orders. The hand that writes is the brain's "pen," whose movements reflect what is going on within the brain itself. In this sense, handwriting analysis is an X-ray of the brain. It enables us to understand what is happening in the body, the mind, and the soul.

The History of Graphology

Graphology is as old as writing itself. For thousands of years people have tried to find a connection between handwriting and personality. The Greek philospher Aristotle and his students dealt with writing and the information concealed within the writing itself. Chinese sages in the East and the Romans in the West all made observations about the shapes of letters.

Graphology has certainly come a long way since then. We are still pioneers, however, in this vast field, where our knowledge is only a drop in the ocean. Even the small amount of knowledge which we possess should be put to full use. Research is carried out; questions are asked, and we make new discoveries at each stage, like a house being built story by story.

The first systematic attempts to describe the relationship between handwriting and personality were made in Italy in the 17th century. Camilio Baldo, a physician and professor of medicine at the University of Bologna, even wrote a book on the subject in 1625. His booklet with the long title *Tratto come una lettra missive cognoscano la natura del scrittore* (*An essay teaching how to examine the character and qualities of the writer from a letter*) did not arouse much interest, and the market was not flooded with additional books.

It was only 150 years later that the Swiss priest Johann Kaspar Luther published a book entitled *Physiognomical Parts*, a section of which dealt with the interpretation of handwriting. Some authorities claim that Goethe supported Luther, contributed some observations of his own, and urged Luther to publish his book. The book was based mainly on intuition, and was written in a rhetorical, rather than scientific, style.

Physiognomical Parts was translated into French about thirty years after its initial publication. As a result of this translation, Abbe Flanhédrin began his empirical research. He attempted to compare personality traits with forms of writing. He concentrated mainly on people he knew, and discovered a connection between certain recurring marks and the character traits of the writers.

We cannot talk about the history of graphology without mentioning Abbé Jean-Hippolite Michon (1806-1881), who followed in the footsteps of his teacher Flanhedrin, and who soon established himself as an expert on handwriting.

Michon coined the term "Graphology," and aroused great interest in the subject in France. Michon was gifted with a visual memory, acute perceptiveness, and a talent for observation. He collected many handwriting samples, and examined them in detail. His basic assumption was that each graphological sign corresponds to a personality trait, and that the absence of a specific sign indicates the lack of its matching trait.

Michon lacked a theoretical foundation. He based his results on individual signs, and did not relate to the total picture.

Modern graphologists do not accept his findings as he interpreted them. We know that no form of expression is unequivocal. There is a little bit of everything in each one of us. The questions which we must ask are, how dominant a quality is, and how it is used by the writer.

Nevertheless, modern graphology is greatly indebted to Abbé Michon, both for the publicity that aroused an interest in graphology, and the thoroughness of observation he introduced into the field. Michon was followed by J. Crépieux-Jamin (1858-1940), who broke the tradition of examining individual signs and related to handwriting **as a whole**, thus giving graphology its modern orientation. He shifted the emphasis from the way someone dotted his i's or crossed his t's to the total picture, while still taking into account the individual elements. Using this methodology, Crepieux-Jamin refuted the view that the absence of a certain sign proves that the corresponding character trait does not exist.

Crépieux-Jamin also conducted extensive research, and excelled in both his scholarship and his practical application of graphology. He classified 175 examples into 7 categories which are still used by modern graphologists. The development of psychology, Freudian psychoanalysis, Gestalt, and other approaches also supported this new, far-reaching direction in graphology. Researchers stopped compiling lists of character traits, and began relating to the writer's entire personality, which was reflected in his handwriting.

At the beginning of the 20th century, German psychologists and psychiatrists became interested in graphology, and they soon produced scholars who laid the groundwork for present-day graphology.

The philosopher Dr. Ludwig Klages (1872-1956) took it upon himself, as his life's work, to develop the science of graphology. Known as the "father of modern graphology," Klages's books are still considered to be the graphologist's Bible.

Klages relied strongly on intuition and on perceiving the character as a whole, similar to the modern psychological approach. His studies still serve as the basis of contemporary methods. Hans Jacoby, whose research was based on Klages's techniques, became the leader in the field after the publication of his book *Handwriting and Sex* in 1932. This book provided the conceptual basis for the later work of Max Pulver. Klages also developed a system of sign ambivalence, determining that any sign may be evidence of both positive and negative qualities, all in accordance with the general picture presented by the handwriting.

Robert Saudek, a native Austrian who spent much of his life in England and the United States, worked with the psychologists June Downey and Frank Freeman. He is responsible for sweeping advances made in the field of graphology. The fact that he lived in different countries helped him to realize that the same language may be taught with slightly different graphic features in each country, despite the letters' seeming to be identical. Saudek established the rule that a graphologist must be familiar with the style someone learned to write before analyzing his handwriting.

Saudek tried to ignore the role of intuition in order to obtain an objective, realistic, and scientific view. Together with Downey and Freeman, Saudek conducted experiments mainly in the area of writing speed, to which we shall again refer later in this book.

Dr. Max Pulver (1889-1952), a Swiss writer, lecturer, and psychologist, included the principles of modern Jungian psychology in his work. He viewed the personality as a multi-layered entity, and rejected the intuitive approach. He wrote a book entitled *The Symbolism of Handwriting*.

Professor Rudolph Pophal, a Hamburg neurologist, established a method of classifying people into categories based on motoric movements. Pophal published several books and other publications in the field of kinetic graphology.

Rhoda Wieser conducted a landmark graphological research, studying the handwriting of criminals for ten years. She discovered what is called the "basic rhythm," and developed a theory concerning criminal tendencies.

Graphology was received with great suspicion in the United States, thrown together with fortune telling, the reading of tea leaves and coffee grounds, and so forth, and has been neglected until the present. It will undoubtedly be a long time before it achieves the same status in America as it already enjoys in Europe, especially in Germany. Graphology is, however, becoming more academically accepted in the United States; Professor Dan Anthony even taught graphology at the New School for Social Research in New York. Several other universities in the United States include courses of graphology in their curriculum. To the best of my knowledge, graphology enjoys a higher status in Israel than in any other country in the world.

Thea Lewinson, Klara Roman, and Nadya Olyanova have written excellent books on graphology, helping to dispel the negative image it has had in the past. Despite all the research that has been conducted, all the books that have been written, and all the lectures that have been given, the science of graphology is still in its infancy, with most of the work still ahead of us.

The Uses of Graphology

Industry and Business

Employers turn to a graphologist when testing the suitability of applicants for a certain position, and when determining the way to make best use of their current employees: making efficient use of their employee's potential, aiding in deciding which employees should be promoted, or choosing the members for a specific team for a project.

Elliot, a man of great intellectual capacity, was not realizing his full potential in the position he filled. I analyzed his handwriting, and found that team work did not suit him. I recommended that his working conditions be changed, so that he could work on his own. The results were astonishing: Elliot soon realized his true potential, much to his and his superiors' satisfaction.

Prospective business partners often consult a graphologist before finalizing their partnership, seeking either support for the planned transaction, or a warning against future hazards.

Two men, Richard and Daniel, were about to sign a contract setting up a large-scale partnership. The day before the agreement was to be finalized, Richard came to see me, bringing samples of his and Daniel's handwriting. According to a superficial examination, the match was a good one. However I found something disturbing, and decided to delay my answer. A second, more thorough analysis revealed that Daniel was two-faced: on the outside, he was friendly, polite, warm, and considerate – which was how Richard saw him. My penetration into a deeper stratum of his handwriting revealed a different side of his personality: greed, criminal tendencies, a desire for fast profits, ruthlessness, and even violence.

Richard was hesitant when I revealed my additional findings. I advised him to postpone signing the contract, and even to hint at the possibility of cancelling the partnership. He followed my advice. Daniel reacted as I had feared: he lost his temper, and became abusive and agressive. Needless to say, the partnership did not materialize.

Criminal Investigations

I am often asked to aid in uncovering forgeries. The truth is that my services are not needed here, but rather those of a handwriting specialist, to conduct a technical analysis. This type of test refers to the form of writing, and not to the character of the writer.

Psychotherapy

Psychologists, psychiatrists, and marriage counselors often ask a graphologist for a second opinion regarding their patients.

Sheila had undergone prolonged treatment in an institution. A diagnosis had been made after six months of treatment, on the basis of several therapists' professional opinions. Before proceeding further with her treatment, the institution's staff requested that I examine a sample of her handwriting. My analysis concurred with their diagnosis, thus enabling the therapists to proceed immediately with the next stage of treatment, shortening Sheila's stay in the institution.

Graphotherapy

This is a relatively recent application of graphology. Someone being counseled by a psychologist or psychiatrist is aided by the graphologist, who teaches him to write in a manner which will facilitate and shorten the therapy.

Family Counseling

The family is a complex system consisting of many relationships: parents, children, each parent with each child, and relationships of members of the immediate family with members of the extended family (e.g. grandparents, aunts and uncles).

People come to the graphologist in order to gain a better understanding of problems in this system: a worried mother wants to understand a son who threatens to leave home, a wife tries to understand her husband's behavior, a father wants to gain a better understanding of his daughter. Graphologists also provide counseling for prospective couples, to determine their suitability for each other, before they wed.

Once I received an urgent phone call from a detective agency. Doris, a teenager, had run away from home. She had left a farewell letter, telling her family they would never see her again. The parents feared the worst.

I examined the letter. It was very long, containing several pages of compressed writing. This indicated vitality, energy, and a more vigorous sexuality than could be expected from a girl of Doris's age. This didn't look like a potential suicide to me. A suicidal person would not write such a long letter, nor would she show such pronounced signs of vitality and strength.

I advised the parents to wait, since I was certain that the girl would contact them. I believed that there were two reasons for her disappearance: she was pregnant and ashamed to admit it, and she had run away with a man her parents did not like.

As I expected, Doris called her parents about five hours later. She had fallen in love with a man many years her senior; tentative conversations with her parents had revealed that they would not approve of such a match. My second deduction about her pregnancy also proved to be true.

Individual Counseling

Graphologists also provide counseling for individuals, for their private needs. These may include improving their self-awareness, aiding in determining the proper direction in studies or employment, or aiding people who have reached a crossroads in their life and who need assistance in determining which path to take.

I met with Jonathan, an older man who was retired, and who did not know how to occupy himself with his free time. His handwriting contained indications of artistic tendencies which had never been realized. Today Jonathan is a successful sculptor, and is quite happy that he discovered and makes use of this newly revealed talent.

Communal Membership

Many communities in Israel that are based on fairly high levels of cooperation and communal involvement use graphological analysis to aid in determining the suitability of membership candidates. These settlements are interested in determining the candidate's suitability to the specific form of settlement, as well as his or her compatability with existing members.

I have a vivid memory of Joshua, who had bought a house in a collective village. Before finalizing Joshua's membership, the village committee asked me to analyze his handwriting. I noted a pattern of mental disturbances. It seemed to me that Joshua was on the verge of a mental breakdown. The members had mixed feelings: their initial reaction toward the applicant had been positive, but they had learned from past experience to rely on graphological analysis. In the end, they rejected his application for membership. Joshua later applied for membership elsewhere. They accepted him. Shortly afterwards the first collective learned that Joshua had suffered a breakdown and had had to be hospitalized.

All these uses for graphology show that the graphologist also fills the role of counselor, and should have psychological training in addition to his knowledge of graphology.

Historical Research

A completely different use of graphology deals with the past. Questions occasionally arise concerning historical figures and historical research may require a close examination of the nature of their personalities. When handwriting samples are available, the graphologist may be helpful in confirming or refuting certain assumptions, thus helping to obtain a more accurate picture of the personality in question.

Common Questions about Graphology

1. *My handwriting is constantly changing, even during the same day. I write differently in the morning and in the evening. How is it possible then that it reflects my character?*

You are different at different times during the day. You are usually more rested in the morning, and more tired at night. This is a constantly recurring fluctuation, and can be seen in the alignment of rows in your handwriting: you'll notice that they rise in the morning, and go down in the evening. These changes in your handwriting reflect changes in your mood; but there are other elements which do not change: your IQ, your parents' influence on you and on your potential. Even if your handwriting is different in the morning than at night, the signs that indicate your constant qualities and characteristics do not change. The

changes which you see are, in most cases, minute, and are not really significant.

2. *What does it mean when I write this type of "t"?*

One letter is not significant enough to determine a characteristic or the structure of a personality. Only an analysis of additional signs and the combination of their meanings can provide a picture of your entire personality.

3. *I began writing "A" this way when I was an adolescent, since my literature teacher wrote this way, and I still write like this. What does this mean?*

This is a common phenomenon. We all try to imitate people during different stages of our development. But we retain only those imitations which suit our own characters. Thus, you will continue to write your "A" this way.

4. *If handwriting is only the result of hand movements, how can you learn so much from it?*

Your assumption is only partially correct. While it is true that handwriting is produced by the motion of your hand, that motion originates in signals sent out by your brain, like any other motor function. If you try to remove a piece of lint from your shirt, or stroke your head, you are engaging in movements whose meaning is determined by the brain (you want to get rid of something unpleasant, you want to be stroked). Psychologists try to interpret these movements, and so do graphologists. They want to discover the specific meaning of the written signs, and through them to analyze the character of the writer. For the graphologist, your handwriting is like an X-ray of what is going on in your brain, both consciously and unconsciously.

5. *Is it possible to reveal a person's future on the basis of his or her handwriting?*

There is no way to predict the writer's future. Handwriting, like other forms of motor movements (see question 4), can only reveal a person's qualities and personality. It cannot predict a person's future, although it does provide a character analysis which may predict how the person will perform in a specific situation of stress, work pressure, etc.

6. *Can diseases be discovered through someone's handwriting?*

Handwriting is like a profile of the entire body. A person suffering from asthma, for example, will write with occasional small interruptions, which can be detected by an experienced graphologist with the help of a magnifying glass. Different parts of letters represent the major divisions of the body: the upper part of the letters "l," "t", and "h" represent the head. The middle part of the body is represented by the middle-zone letters ie; "a", "c", "e", "o", while the legs are represented by the lower parts of the letters "g," "y," and "f." It is a well-known fact that a person who is not completely well unconsciously holds the pen for a split second longer on the part of the letter which corresponds to the afflicted part of his body. This produces a small spot, visible to the trained eye through a magnifying glass. The graphologist can thereby detect diseases in their initial stages. The same is true of pregnancy: even before you receive the results of a lab test, a small spot will appear in the appropriate section of the letters you write (see p. *249* for more destails).

7. *Does handwriting reveal a person's sex and age?*

We all have "masculine" and "feminine" traits, that have nothing to do with physiology. In our society, women have developed qualities which have always been considered to be masculine, and they are in fact more "masculine" than their mothers; men, on the other hand, have acquired "feminine" properties such as intuition or dependence. Although we can speak of a more "masculine" or a more "feminine" handwriting, handwriting usually reflects an individual's character and personality, rather than sex. I usually ask for some information prior to conducting an examination of handwriting, including the sex of the individual.

Peter's handwriting does not give away his sex. He is a man, working in a "feminine" profession – a cosmetician in a beauty salon. His behavior and movements are feminine, he is emotional and sensitive, and has other traits traditionally regarded as feminine. His sexual orientation is also directed more towards men than towards women.

The second handwriting sample belongs to Mata Hari, who is still considered to be a very feminine woman. Her handwriting appears strong, rigid, and masculine. There is no doubt that she had many "masculine" characteristics.

I have just realized that seven days ago was exactly five years ago that I moved to this wonderful city... San Francisco...

Peter

Mata Hari

are such
saucy fellows
but so beautiful
The energy problem
seems to be uppermost

Carol

a very sketchy schooling, in fact none at
all in the early years owing to war and
revolution   After much excitement most
of which I have forgotten we settled to
a normal (fairly) humdrum existence in

Nina

Now let's look at three more handwriting samples, as we try to answer the age question. The first two, those of Carol and Nina, look young and fresh. Carol is 81 years old. Her handwriting is large, spontaneous, natural, and swift. She is completely independent in all her action and takes good care of her appearance. Her handwriting shows us her strength and inexhaustible vigor. Nina is 73 years old. Judging from her handwriting, she appears to be somewhat childish. The alternations in her handwriting are more appropriate for an adolescent than an elderly woman. Linda's handwriting also looks childish. Although she is about 60 years old, you can see from her handwriting that she is as naive as any 16-year-old might be.

your welcome letter, time seems to go by so fast and I have been extremly busy.

Thank you for the viewcard and the lovely stamps I am enclosing our latest issue out last week, they depict the year of the disabled.

You certainly had a marvellous holiday and so many lovely memories to store for future

Linda

8. What gives you the right to analyze other people's handwriting?

I am often asked this question, but not as frequently as in the past, since public acceptance of graphology is on the rise. The experience of many years has strengthened graphology's credibility, and has shown that it is a precision tool with which one can diagnose character, talents, potential, and personality structure.

There is nothing secretive about graphology. Many "Wanted" ads in the newspapers request handwritten applications, so that the applicant can be examined by a graphologist. Most job applicants are aware of this, and agree to it by submitting samples of their handwriting. The application forms of many corporations explicitly state that the application will undergo graphological analysis. A personnel director told me quite frankly that before he knew me, he used to accept people for work on the basis of a personal interview. He was candid enough to admit that he rejected applicants if he did not like their footwear or hair style, even if everything else seemed to meet the job's requirements.

Graphology has become accepted by psychiatrists and psychologists as well. Graphology helps them shorten lengthy observation and treatment periods, especially when there is a need to explain internal, otherwise indetectable processes. In fact, we all seem to have a need to analyze people's characters, but we usually do this without the right tools, and without any objective basis. Who doesn't talk about the boss being in a bad mood this morning, or the neighbor who always screams at her children, or curious friends who love to peep into everyone's kitchen? Everyone uses expressions like, "She is depressed, she looks so thin," or "His thin lips are a sign of cruelty," and even pseudopsychological terminology, such as "Susan is a schizophrenic," "Tom is a paranoid," etc. Every day you hear dozens of psychiatric diagnoses of, and by, other drivers on the road. All these statements and judgments are made on the basis of our "knowledge" gleaned from the newspapers, stereotyped. Graphologists, on the other hand, do possess reliable tools, which have been refined over the course of many decades. The body of evidence concerning the accuracy of graphology grows by leaps and bounds, from day to day. If we have this tool, it would be a crime not to use it.

The one remaining question is that of professional ethics, or the possibility of using handwriting in a dishonest manner. This is the same problem faced by other disciplines dealing with human beings, such as medicine and psychology. Even when preventative measures are taken, such as the Hippocratic Oath for doctors, the danger still remains. This issue is especially sensitive in the field of graphology, since anyone who has read a book or two on the subject can declare himself a "graphologist." The work of such amateurs may cause great harm to those "analyzed" by them, and blemishes the reputation of the entire discipline. In order to prevent such dangers, it is important that the novice graphologist work under the guidance of an experienced and trustworthy expert. He should start by analyzing his own handwriting and that of people close to him, and only gradually move on to the analysis of other people's handwriting, while still under the watchful eye of an experienced graphologist.

9. Is graphology a science?

This is still a moot point. Allport and Vernon, well-known psychologists and devotees of modern graphology, wrote in 1933 that graphology was met with skepticism in America, while it had many followers in Europe. Americans rejected graphology as a science because it has not been supported by a sufficiently large body of empirical and statistical proof. Making matters even worse, many American graphologists are former fortune tellers or those dealing in the occult, a fact which emphasizes its negative image and prevents people from taking it seriously.

Attitudes towards graphology are markedly different in Europe. In Switzerland, for example, graphology is studied in universities within their psychology departments.

In the final analysis, you need scientific methods in order to analyze handwriting, although the final integration of all the facts must be made on an intuitive basis. It is clear that a great deal of scientific research will be devoted to testing graphology in the future. This question of the validity of graphology is similar to those asked about all the social and behavioral sciences, and the answer is also the same: a resounding yes.

Symbolism in Handwriting

Writing existed long before pen and paper were invented and it has undergone a long process of changes since then, with the initial drawings of animals and objects turning into abstract symbols.

The earliest stage of writing dates back to the drawings and symbols of primitive man on cave walls. After this, people wrote on stone tablets, and then on papyrus and on scrolls. We find the following "pictures" in drawings which served as writing, and which have been revealed by archaeologists:

house   *mountain*   *bull*

Egyptian hieroglyphics, or picture-writing, included symbols such as a cup — which stood for

"hospitality" (see the section on the garland in chapter on connective forms, p. *188*).

There is a strong connection between symbols and writing in the modern world, but we cannot, of course, analyze character only on the basis of symbols. Symbols can serve us as an additional tool, confirming phenomena and qualities which we have already revealed.

We are taught from earliest childhood that Good (God, sun, Heaven) is above us, while Evil (the grave, hell, the Devil) is below us. Without even thinking, we talk of having "ups and downs" – the "ups" are good moods, and the "downs" are bad moods. Moving ahead is synonymous with moving up; when we think of depression, tiredness, and failure, we automatically associate this with sinking down.

This same division applies to our handwriting. The upper region is the one associated with values, yearnings, and principles; the lower region, on the other hand, is linked to depression, crises, and the instincts.

The traditional symbols for man and woman also reflect this division (as well as the value judgments assigned by society): the arrow of the male symbol points up, while the female symbol has a line pointing down.

The father was always considered as the parent responsible for the education of his children, while the mother was identified with more earthly needs: cooking, clothing and cleaning of the house.

Symbolic language, the language portrayed by symbols, is essentially similar to body language. The following handwriting samples will help us gain a better understanding of the relationship between the language of writing, body movements and agreed-upon symbols.

This is Margaret's handwriting. She drew hearts during the period she was in love.

Quand je suis

Margaret

Alice's handwriting, on the other hand, includes a reversed heart in her signature. This type of writing often expresses a disappointing love life.

Love
Alice

Alice

People who connect t's in different parts of a word with one line have mathematical minds, like games, and seek intellectual stimulation.

Indilute

In our next two samples you can easily detect dollar signs ($). This often appears in the handwriting of people who are involved in financial affairs, or who are money-oriented.

P.S. Just

I live at 175 N.J. I am a stock

My friend Ruth was a designer of theatre sets who went into real estate, and became very money-oriented. One evening when I visited her, I went to the telephone to make a call and found this doodle on her note pad:

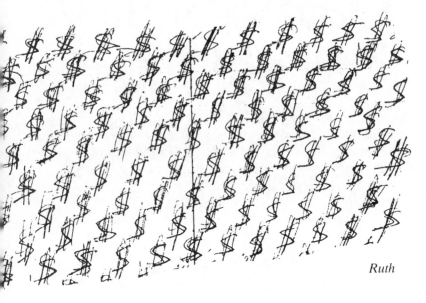

Ruth

Nahum is an Israeli who entered the import-export business. Most of his business dealings are with American firms. At the same time that his life took this new direction, dollar signs began to appear in his writing, even though he writes in a language other than English.

Nahum

The handwriting by Zico Graziani, a conductor, contains letters which resemble musical notes. Despite the fact that the sample was written in Bulgarian, we can still analyze it according to our rules, without understanding, or even being able to read, the contents of the sample.

Zico Graziani

Bill's handwriting also contains letters which clearly resemble notes. These forms are quite typical of people who write music; their hands are used to writing musical symbols.

Bill

Clifford, a pianist adds a creative touch to his
hanwriting: by drawing notes.

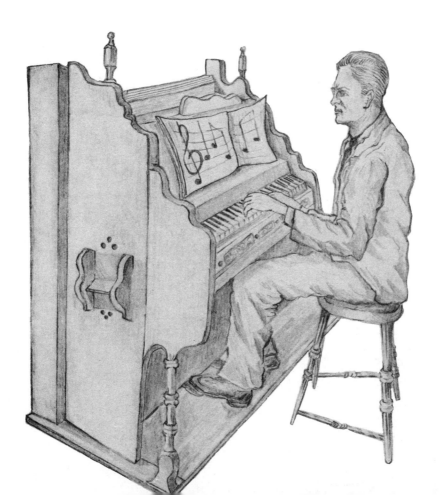

Clifford

36

Ann's pregnancy is very advanced, and she gives her letters "R" and "F" a stomach whose size graphically reflects her physical condition. You can see in the letter "R" the shape of a fetus, connected by an umbilical cord. Ann was unable to conceive for eight years, and now her handwriting shows us the intensity of her involvement with her pregnancy.

Right-handed

Age

Female

Ann

- Étranger en Israel, parlant peu la langue, aidé de plus par une formation militaire, je pense que je peux m'adapter assez facilement à la vie communautaire du kibb et que je m'y plairai.

Claude

Even religion leaves its marks in people's handwriting. Claude is a very devout Catholic; look at all the cross signs in his handwriting.

People who deal with figures often include numbers in their handwriting, as in this sample:

[Handwritten letter by Daniel Defoe]

Daniel Defoe

Quite unconsciously, authors often leave traces of the subjects of their books in their handwriting. Look at this sample of handwriting by Daniel Defoe, the author of *Robinson Crusoe*. The ocean waves surrounding Defoe's hero appear in every line of Defoe's handwriting.

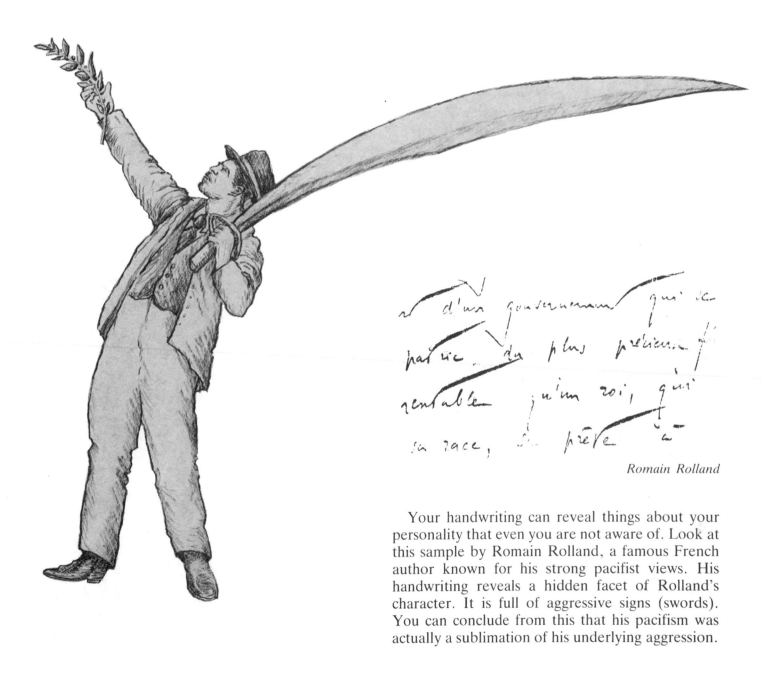

Romain Rolland

Your handwriting can reveal things about your personality that even you are not aware of. Look at this sample by Romain Rolland, a famous French author known for his strong pacifist views. His handwriting reveals a hidden facet of Rolland's character. It is full of aggressive signs (swords). You can conclude from this that his pacifism was actually a sublimation of his underlying aggression.

Now let's look at the handwriting of a famous historical figure – Otto von Bismarck. Bismarck (1815-1898) entered political life at the age of 32 and became the Prime Minister of Prussia 15 years later, after having served as a diplomat in Russia and France. He is known for creating the second German Reich, holding the title of Chancellor. The British historians Fisher and Taylor claim that Bismarck's aggressive foreign policy was instrumental in worsening relations between the Great Powers and that this caused a worldwide stress situation.

Otto von Bismarck

We find that his writing clearly reflects stubbornness and competitiveness, the outstanding characteristics of Bismarck's personality, along with a domineering trait and signs of megalomania and schizophrenia.

The dots formed like circles indicate his hallucinations and inability to face reality.

His sharp, pointed, strokes indicate aggressiveness – they look like a knife ready to strike.

The first letter in this quote is disproportionately high, and forms the shape of an ellipse. This reveals his struggle against his lack of self-confidence, compensated for by dramatic behavior, showing off, and his determination to best everyone else and master the world.

Look at the repetition of the first letter in his signature. This shows a schizophrenic tendency, once again indicating his struggle against his lack of self-confidence, expressing itself this time in megalomania, a mental delusion marked by feelings of grandeur or the belief that one is the Almighty.

The Shapes of Letters and Their Meanings

Geometrical letter forms such as squares and triangles in the upper zone indicate an interest in building and a constructive mind.

The peculiar shape and extra loops indicate childish traits and attachment to a maternal figure.

The first part of the letter is out of proportion in comparison to its second part. This signifies ambition, as if to say, "The sky's the limit."

The wavy line crossing the "t" indicates a jester or clown, with a sense of humor, funloving.

Embellishment and inflated letters show vanity and self-admiration.

A mushroom-like arcade means insecurity and self-defense.

A letter formed like a clef shows musical tendencies.

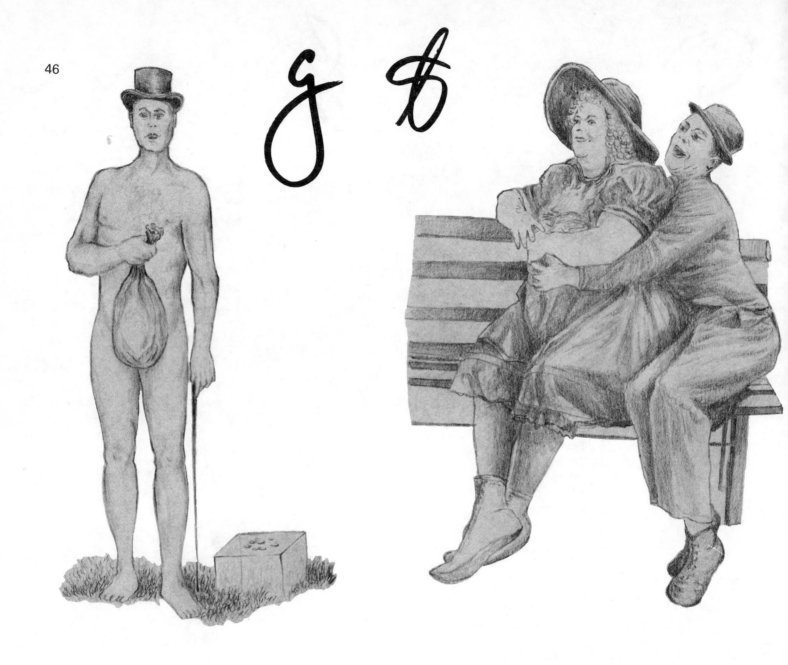

46

Long inflated loops, in the lower zone, indicate possessiveness, greediness, and sensuality. This looks like a moneybag.

The knotted small "t" reveals the desire for a close relationship.

The unique formation of this "L" shows an artistic inclination.

The crossbar of the "t," broadening towards the end, shows an aggresive attitude.

The Process of Learning How to Write

Writing begins with speech.

The child hears voices and words, which he remembers and tries to imitate. He uses his lips, tongue, and palate, which make it possible to produce sounds. The movements, the pauses during speech, speed, volume, and fluency all differ from child to child, and from family to family.

The sounds which the child finally produces are those which he has selected from among a large range of phonetic possibilities, choosing the sounds which he finds to be meaningful and easily pronounced. These sounds will become part of the child's permanent phonetic inventory.

Learning to write follows a similar pattern. Just as arbitrary, meaningless sounds are the first step on the way to coherent speech, so is the baby's scribbling on anything in his way. When a baby holds a pen or crayon for the first time, he tries it out on a nearby table, sheet of paper, or wall, without any preconceived form or direction.

Of course there is a difference between the two learning processes: the child learns to speak at home, while writing (as opposed to drawing) is taught in an organized, institutional manner, in school. In both cases, however, the first stimuli come from the parents: they are the source of the first words the child hears, and they provide the first positive reinforcement for the sounds he makes. In the same manner, the parents are the first ones to give their child writing instruments, and encouragement in using them (if he sticks to paper, and not to the living room's walls...).

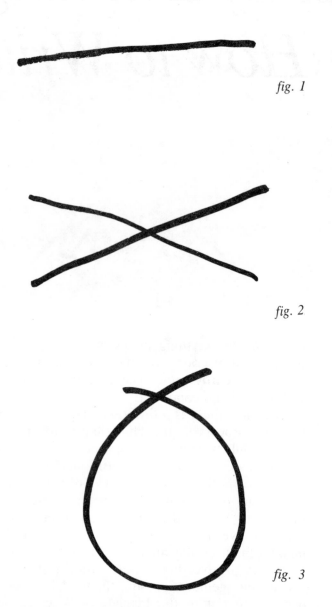

fig. 1

fig. 2

fig. 3

The first stage in a child's graphic activity is the scribbling stage, at about the age of two. The child has not yet learned how to control his drawing, and he moves his pencil across the paper in a mostly random manner. As the child develops, his scribbling becomes more controlled and refined. This initial stage is common to both writing and drawing.

In the next stage, the child succeeds in drawing a line – usually a horizontal line, from left to right (see fig. 1). This achievement makes him feel as proud as when he said "Mommy" or "Daddy" for the first time.

Some parents or day-care center teachers may examine this "creation" and say, "But you still have a lot of room left on the paper!" This is a mistake. A mother whose child has just said "Mommy" for the first time wouldn't tell him that he still has a lot of words to learn. A positive reaction, such as a hug or an expression of pleasure, will encourage the child to continue in his explorations. A line that "came out well" is a major creative success for the small child.

In the next stage, the child draws two lines, a horizontal one and a vertical one (see fig. 2).

At approximately three years of age, the child usually tries to draw specific objects. He attempts to draw a circle (fig. 3).

At about the age of four, the child makes his first attempts to draw people (fig. 4). Drawing people is a great challenge at this age. As you can see in drawings made during this stage, the child's perception is inclusive. The head includes the body, with the arms and legs extending from this roundish shape. Children do not relate to details at this stage, the proportions are still wrong, and a lot of elements (eyes, ears, clothes, and so forth) are lacking. The process of completing these missing details continues throughout the later stages of the child's development.

A six-year-old draws children and adults, and outlines their clothes (fig. 5). This creates the impression that the clothes are transparent. It is only at a later stage that the child begins to fill in the clothes with colors or lines.

In certain types of mental illness, the patients lose some of their ability to communicate. They may revert to a childish state, and express themselves by means of their drawings.

fig. 4

fig. 5

Personality

We define personality as the total of all the inherited and acquired properties which characterize a person, and distinguish him from all other people. This biography is not static, but dynamic, and even volatile at times. Our personality undergoes constant change. We always receive new stimuli, increase our knowledge, and develop emotionally. Human beings are not simply the sum of all their qualities; we often find two people possessing the same qualities, but whose behavior is completely different.

When you have learned to analyze handwriting samples, you will discover that people with identical qualities, such as their intelligence and degree of sociability, may function intellectually and socially in completely different ways, due to emotional inhibitions, lack of self-confidence, impatience, or compulsive behavior.

You will learn of the importance of the interaction between qualities. In order to analyze handwriting, you will also require a psychological and scientific basis, as well as a great deal of intuition and the ability to see the overall picture.

There is nothing mysterious about intuition. Intuition is simply the ability of an intelligent and sensitive person to plant the kernels of information and knowledge and to reap them at the appropriate moment, without being able to explain how he arrived at his conclusion.

Although people do respond differently and each personality is unique in its own ways, psychologists and graphologists have attempted to classify individuals into personality types. I've always felt that this typology, or division into types, is somewhat forced, and certainly artificial. Classification into types is the beginning of every science (such as classification of plants, rocks, etc.) but on top of everything else people tend to classify others according to their prior experience. Human beings seem to have a need to belong to groups. They often find that someone reminds them of someone in their family or a neighbor. It is important to remember however that those classifications into types have their limits, since, in the final analysis, there are no "pure" types. Each human being is a complex of different characteristics, which in turn form a combination of several "pure types." We must therefore avoid generalizations and stereotypes when engaging in graphological analysis.

You will however find that those classifications into types are useful in the initial stages of handwriting observation. These typologies provide us with a general framework for describing universal human characteristics. But you should never rely on typology alone when drawing your conclusions. Your analysis must be in-depth, based on a thorough study of the facts which you find in the handwriting itself.

Human personality is an extremely complex issue, and man has devoted much study to the subject over the millenia. Let's look at a few of the major contributors to the study of the personality, and their respective typologies.

Hippocrates

About 2,500 years ago, the Greek physician Hippocrates, known as the Father of Medicine, developed his theory of human types. He assumed that human character was determined by bodily fluids (blood, bile, phlegm, and saliva), and divided mankind into four types:

The **choleric** temperament (green bile, from the Greek *chole*, "bile"), symbolized as fire, being hot, dry, quick, and strong. The characteristic properties of this temperament are: emotionality, irascibility and easiness of conciliation, perseverance, profound thought, strictness, practical sense, oversensitivity, authoritarianism, restlessness, impulsiveness, and directly fighting obstacles, instead of avoiding them.

The **sanguine** temperament (red bile, from the Latin *sanguis*, "blood"), symbolized as air – hot, humid, quick, and weak. Characteristic properties: hot and lively temperament, alertness, vitality, love of life, great emotionality, talkativeness, sincerity, readiness to compromise, opportunism, superficiality, lack of perseverance.

The **melancholic** temperament (black bile, from the Greek *melas* "black" and *chole* "bile"), symbolized as earth – cold, dry, slow, and strong. Characteristic properties: lack of emotion, responsibility, a sense of duty, feeling of inferiority, lack of self-confidence, self-imposed isolation, idealism, slowness, limited ability to carry out actions.

The **phlegmatic** temperament (white bile, from the Greek *phlegma*, "saliva, white fluid"), symbolized as water – moist, slow, and weak. Characteristic properties: passivity, lack of emotionality, perseverance, laziness, fatalism, devotion, loyalty, responsibility, and rigidity.

René Le Senne

Dr. René Le Senne, a French psychologist and philosopher, adapted the theory of Hippocrates and revised the classification system of two Dutch psychologists, Heymans and Wiersma, whose work is called the Dutch school of psychology.

Le Senne established a system of three essentials differentiating character. He identified eight personality types, each consisting of a different combination of these factors. Let's look at each of these factors and personality types, and the way these characteristics are expressed in handwriting.

Emotivity (E) – non-Emotivity (nE)

Each event, thought, and sensation produces a reaction in the individual, according to the subject's degree of sensitivity. This reaction is expressed in actions, gestures, or words. Everyone, of course, experiences some emotion. For our purposes, however, non-Emotivity refers to a limited amount of emotional response. Emotivity refers to a proneness to emotion, with the slightest of causes producing heavy responses, such as happiness, tears, or outbursts of temper.

Activity (A) – non-Activity (nA)

This category does not refer to movement or action, but rather to a *natural disposition* for activity. The Active type constantly seeks to keep himself busy. The non-Active type acts only in response to external causes, and does not do more than he has to. He will always find excuses to delay the moment of action.

The Active type is stimulated by obstacles; he views them as stepping-stones. The non-Active type is discouraged by obstacles, which block his ability to act. He is tortured by self-doubt, and falls prey to pessimism and stagnation. The Active type, however, faces problems head on, and tries to solve them, full of enthusiasm and confidence.

Primary and Secondary responsiveness

Responsiveness has two poles, a **Primary**, immediate reaction, and a **Secondary**, long-term, reaction.

Le Senne illustrates the difference between these two reactions with the example of a professor who sees that the wall clock shows that he does not have enough time to finish his lecture before the class ends. The Primary effect would be for the professor to speak more quickly, so that he could finish his lecture before being cut off by the bell. The Secondary, long-term effect would have the professor change the manner in which he would deliver his lectures in the future, so that he would not be caught short by the bell again.

Let's think of another example. Suppose you felt insulted by someone. You answer back immediately, without thinking about the consequences. This is a Primary reaction. If you were to go home or to work, and think about the insult scenario for a long time, perhaps even for weeks or months, and then talk again to the other person about what happened, this would be a Secondary reaction, characterized by long-term pondering and responses to the original event.

People who are strongly affected and respond immediately to stimuli are called "primaries". They are more impulsive, with intense, but short-lived, reactions. Those people who are dominated by past or future considerations are called "secondaries." They are more repressed and inhibited, and seem to be more reflective than the primaries. They build complicated links to the past and the future. They are less spontaneous, but seem to have deeper perceptions than the primaries.

Choleric
(EAP – emotive-active-primary)

This dynamic combination produces an individual who is sensitive, enthusiastic, and very enterprising. As vital as he is demanding, he has a strong appetite for physical pleasures. He lives life to the fullest, living for the moment at hand. His emotivity gives him sympathy for his fellow man. He deals well with the public.

The Activity component makes him a doer, one who is always happy to be of service. He makes bold and optimistic plans, and executes tasks effectively and promptly.

The Primary component, on the other hand, causes him to forget past experiences, so he learns little from them. His opinions and statements are inconsistent. He prefers dropping an undertaking and starting all over again rather than enduring postponement.

The Choleric type makes a brilliant speaker, because he loves the sound of his own voice. He seeks to be in the public eye, and he is a leader and a pacesetter. He is drawn to politics, and enjoys a fight that tests his power. He also may seek to express himself as painter, poet, or writer. He is too hasty, however, and is unwilling to spend time on details.

He is optimistic and happy, radiates good will and strength, which make him popular.

He is able to adjust quickly, even spontaneously. He is efficient, down to earth, and likes to engage in different subjects at the same time. He is constantly on the go, works in his free time, and hates to postpone anything. He intends to reach the goals he sets for himself.

Characteristics of Choleric handwriting:
strong, uniform pressure, without exaggerations
speedy writing
direct connections (usually without a straight line)
no margins; a feeling of being as one with the paper
centrifugal and centripetal tendencies, developed middle-zone, significant up and down strokes
lack of attention to regularity
irregular letter size
spaces between letters, wide right margins
angular writing (the angles are not even, but if they are present, they do not appear to be compulsive)

Dear Anna

I enclose handwriting for four people who have applied for the position of Security Officer.

Dany is coming to London next Wednesday and could bring the analyses with him

You also have one for a — I need all of these for next Thursday (July 5th)

Thank you

Handwriting of a Choleric type

Nervous
(EnAP – emotive-non-active-primary)

He is more susceptible to nervous and mental disorders than any other type. Many artists belong to this category.

He has strong emotions. Now is what counts for him. He has a subjective attitude towards the world. He has no self-control, indulges himself, and changes jobs, professions, and lovers. He has no memory of events, and requires constant stimulation. He may be deceitful, and may pretend to be something he is not. He thrives on compliments.

Characteristics of Nervous type handwriting
uneven movement
unessential up-strokes, exaggerations, impulsive sudden irregularities, small-sized letters followed by the same letters written larger
impulsive movement
extremely simplified signature
irregular, undisciplined sizes (a very important sign)
change of speed (another important sign)
disorderly arrangement
inconsistent and disorderly lines, margins, and slant
irregular connections; hesitation instead of decisiveness
centrifugal strokes
speed
much movement; inconsistency; never making a strong impression (like someone blown by the wind)

The truth of handwriting is one
that has an age- and
validity, & a certain intrigue.
Some people believe that the

Handwriting of a Nervous type

Sanguine
(nEAP – non-emotive-active-primary)

Emotion plays little, if any, role in his life. Common sense is dominant; thanks to the Active-Primary combination, he is realistic, practical, and quick to grasp opportunities. He is usually good at making money, and likes the pleasures that money can buy.

The Primary component supplies vivacity. He adapts himself to current needs and seeks immediate results, not distant goals. He chooses his words carefully and employs convincing logic. He is a good diplomat, a skilful tactician, and successful as a lawyer, businessman, or government official. His lack of emotionalism prevents him from getting excited, even when everyone around him is losing their heads. He is an ideal mediator.

He is not very sensitive, passionate, or introspective, yet he is alert to, and dependent upon, the world around him. This causes him to align his own interests with those of the general public.

When in love he is always in control, and he is more physical than romantic. He is inconsistent, a realist, persistent, objective, self-disciplined, and a good observer. He is pleasant and kind, but uninvolved. This leads to his being sarcastic and cynical, but not out of weakness.

He is liberal politically. He is egotistic, does not like children or animals. He is correct with his inferiors, and has a good sense of orientation. He is good at sports and has drive and courage.

Characteristics of Sanguine type handwriting
legibility
changing slant
good proportions, like schoolchild printing
no exaggerations
simplified natural writing, essential strokes
irregular upper length
quick, but not uncontrolled, writing
mostly unconnected letter groupings
basic line a bit wavy
small variations in lettering
easy, moderate speed; good, even, rather strong, pressure

I am presently writing an article for presentation of the American Psychiatric Association meetings in Dallas, Texas in May, 1985. The article deals with the present state of surgery as it applies

Handwriting of a Sanguine type

Impassioned
(EAS – emotive-active-secondary)

The most tense of all the types. Emotivity provides his driving energy, and his Activity makes this an effective force. His Secondary component adds method and continuity to his efforts. This combination makes him the strongest of all the types. Many generals belong to this category.

His capacity and power make him the most ambitious of all the eight types. He does everything in order to achieve his goals, exhibiting great perseverance, courage, and tenacity, but without being dogmatic or inflexible. He is highly adaptable to changing circumstances.

He strives for greatness, for an ideal, or simply to attain a goal, gladly sacrificing his own interests and comfort, and even his life. His habits border on the ascetic (the top executive having a sandwich at his desk for lunch is a good example). Food, drink or sex are of no importance to him. He does not desire material benefits. His capacity for work is tremendous, since this is his main interest in life. He does not "waste" much time on sleep or relaxation. He uses other people to attain his goals, and expects others to follow his example; this type is often the executive who wears out his employees or the general who does not hesitate to sacrifice men to win a battle. He is a fanatic, for whom the ends justify the means. Authoritative, persistent and impatient, he is motivated to overcome obstacles, and never gives up. He is practical and knows how to get down to essentials; he has a broad perspective, and dislikes detail. He is gifted with a correct perception of reality and a good memory.

On the other hand, when he is not blinded by ambition, he is virtuous, serious, compassionate, patriotic, unpretentious, and unselfish. He prefers to act within a social context. He would sacrifice his life for the common good. He is not interested in sports, and has no artistic inclinations. He likes history. He empathizes with others, likes to help other people, and can show kindness to his subordinates.

He is neither pretentious nor vain. He is himself at all times. He likes cleanliness and order. He feels deprived when not in command. He has to be responsible for everything. His orders must be obeyed so that he can reach his goals. He is demanding and strict when in action, but considerate at other times. He helps those who obey him and destroys those who do not.

Characteristics of Impassioned type handwriting
very definitely connected (interwoven)
rightward trend
wide letters
dynamic writing
quick script, centrifugality
tendency to threadlike writing
not particularly regular, but without striking irregularities which disturb the picture as a whole
homogeneity
systematic
even, mostly heavy, pressure

It was really very nice to see Hannah again in London. We all wish her very well in her new venture in England and in America. 'It will not be easy - but to build something worth while is never easy.

We all have learned a great deal about graphology and it quite frankly amazes us all. It is a science that none of us here tonight understand — but we have a great deal

Handwriting of an Impassioned type

Sentimental
(EnAS – emotive-non-active-secondary)

He is especially sensitive, receptive, and impressionable. Since his Secondary component gives these qualities an in-depth and long-lasting dimension, he is the most vulnerable of all the types. He can be easily, and deeply, hurt, and avoids sorrowful situations. He needs protection. The Secondary component is also responsible for his being moral, inhibited, serious, loyal, and a person with lofty aspirations. His inactivity makes him feel impotent to realize these aspirations, so he is dissatisfied with himself; this festers like an open wound, causing him to become a vindictive enemy, the most irreconcilable of men.

His dominant traits are his changing moods and depression. He is constantly worried, and never satisfied with himself. He is an introvert. He reacts slowly and cannot deal with many things at the same time. He wants much more than he can achieve. He has a selective set of values, and views the world subjectively. He is easily bored, and can burst with no prior warning. He is insecure, and does not believe in the future or in himself. He has no manual dexterity. He tends not to find immediate solutions.

Characteristics of Sentimental type handwriting
good organization
words crowded together, good connections between letters
small, heavy, agitated writing
many corrections, not smooth
illegible (he tries to write nicely, but cannot maintain the effort)
inconsistent proportions and irregular letter height, spacing, pressure
thin forms, disfigured letters
contradictory, slow writing – uses many forms for the same letter

Aim - to write a contract for social studies.
① each student is expected to come to class
prepared with the necessary materials and Be
seated in his or her own seat propity
② In order to speak in class students must
raise their hand and wait to Becalied on.
③ each person is responsible for the cleanliness of
the area - this includes floors, desks, sink areas.
④ The Bathrooms are not a home away from
home. no students is to make his privat
needs a matter of class publicity, Plan ahead
(Recess & Lunch times)
⑤ students have been provided with storag
areas, all other surfaces are community
property and of limits to Private goats.
please remove all items at the end of class
⑥ Arrival into the Area does not need to
resemble a cattle stempede furnitur is to

Handwriting of a Sentimental type

Phlegmatic
(nEAS – non-emotive-active-secondary)

Sensitive, but does not become excited; even-tempered, not spontaneous or compulsive. His Emotive and Secondary components make him calm, impassive, self-controlled, and sober in his speech and behavior. He is unpretentious and knows his limitations and those of his goals.

He possesses integrity, and truthfulness, has a strong sense of duty and much respect for the law, and is thrifty, punctual, broadminded, and sticks to his principles.

He decides after careful examination, and goes into detail without losing his sense of proportion. He usually engages in intellectual pursuits, and he prefers theory and scientific research to practical work. He keeps busy, is extremely methodical in his work, and lacks creativity. He is patient and persevering in all his undertakings.

Characteristics of Phlegmatic type handwriting
legibility, even calligraphical forms
no exaggerations
good proportions, clarity prevails
nothing out of the ordinary
no artistic or ornate forms
restrained, homogenous, well-organized writing
basic line a bit ascending
garlands and angles
vital, not static, writing; inner dynamism
some (restrained) centrifugal strokes in the upper zone
wide writing
strokes have dynamic, not monotonous, pressure;
clean strokes

Characteristics missing in Phlegmatic type handwriting.
unevenness, tangled base line
bad proportions and arrangement
quick script
unfinished sentences, words, or letters;
corrections or threads
exaggerations
entanglements
unnecessary ornaments
complicated, embellished signature
sudden changes in pressure
letters suspended in the middle, not reaching the base line

Well, your doll has finally been wrapped up and ready to be sent out
t. morrow. Thks for the 3 $'s you've so Kindly help me to subsidise the
mailing of the doll. If the parcel isn't too heavy and expensive. I'll
try to send it off by Air. Otherwise, hope you won't mind waiting if I had
to send it by sea. As soon as you have receive the doll, please
Kindly write and let me Know of it, okay?

Yeah!! Isn't it gorgeous to hear that you have intended to travel
to the Far East in August. Don't miss coming to Singapore, the Garden
of the East. You will fall in love with the queeness and cleanliness
of this island.

You enquired about Ayer Itam Temper in Penang. Well, it is actually
a very ancient temple whose the people worship their Idols there.
It is a house of offering prayers to God, and also a tourist attract..
How is your health these days? Do consult a physician if you
are not feeling too good. Health is most important in our lives. L

Handwriting of a Phlegmatic type

Amorphous
(nEnAP – non-emotive-non active-primary)

Character description: Lacking feeling for others and interests in external things; primarily subject to his own organic needs. He is extravagant and wasteful, with a strong inclination towards gambling. He is self-indulgent, and always ready to yield to temptation to satisfy his physical desires. He likes food and drink as well as sex and neglects his duties; although he may have great intellectual potential, he does not make use of it. He lacks any practical sense, and is too insensitive to be easily discouraged. He is negligent, lazy, and indecisive. His Primary component gives him a certain degree of spontaneity of expression, aiding him in all interpretive art (acting, music, dancing, sculpture, etc.). He however procrastinates. He does not value punctuality, ideas, or patriotism. He is malleable, and takes direction from others; he can only be animated by an external force. He does not have any proper influence of his own, and easily adapts himself. He is calm, and does not react.

It is very difficult to identify this type.

Characteristics of Amorphous type handwriting
wide writing and spacing
rounded and simple (not enriched) letters
even left margins
bad proportions, irregular sizes
slant changes
legible, but irritating to the eye
threads
centrifugal strokes, side by side with centripetal
weak strokes
struggle to attain homogenous form
soft, rubbery writing, slow and irregular (as if the writer is tired of writing)

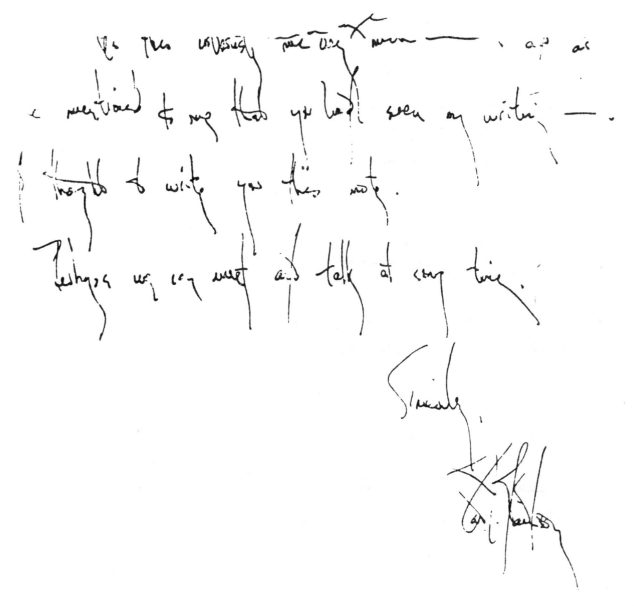

Handwriting of an Amorphous type

Apathetic
(nEnAS – non-emotive-non-active-secondary)

Talks little, and laughs even less. He has no active internal life, and is extremely empty. His preference for solitude is motivated by his total indifference to everybody and everything; he dislikes both children and animals.

He is honest, faithful, sober, prudent, orderly, excessively thrifty, keeps his sensuality under control, and sticks firmly to his principles. His strength is expressed in resistance, rather than in active willpower. He therefore lacks the perseverance needed to accomplish; he adheres stubbornly to his beliefs and opinions.

He is clearly introverted, with melancholic tendencies. Although he is resentful and stubborn, he possesses no ambition. He is not moody, and nothing excites him. He is not prone to hysteria or mental illness.

Characteristics of Apathetic type handwriting
rigid strokes, no vitality
slow writing
short ending strokes for "a" and "d"
suspended letters, do not reach the base line
high level of legibility
well-proportioned
unoriginal forms
well-placed punctuation, according to learned standard forms
well-arranged, regular forms

Quick Handwriting

Slow Handwriting

Nous vous réservons donc une chambre
du 10 au 17 février, et une autre
pour votre secrétaire du 13 au 17 février.
Si vous préférez être ensemble, ce sera
possible aussi. A très bientôt donc.
De tout cœur. S? Marie Bruno

Handwriting of an Apathetic type

Carl Jung

Carl Jung made a distinction between the introverted and extroverted personality types, a distinction which is still used today.

The pure introvert is indecisive, reflective, closed, uncommunicative, and tends to be defensive and suspicious.

The pure extrovert is basically open, communicative, enthusiastic, easily involved and adaptable, and ready to experiment with new situations, without fear.

Basing ourselves on Jung's approach, we can draw the following parallels between these basic types and the characteristic graphological features of their handwriting.

Introvert

Character properties: Activity and judgment determined by internal, rather than external, factors, limited connection with other people and the environment, problems in communicating, egocentricity, alienation, escapist attitude, introspective. Highly imaginative and original thinker, poor adaptability, complex personality.

Graphological characteristics: Narrow and uneven left margin, broad right margin, broad and irregular spacing between words and lines, slow writing, small and narrow lettering, garlands and angles, small irregularities in length, uneven (rather weak) pressure. Disconnected, rhythmical stroke, upright or leftward slant, stressed upper zone.

Extrovert

Character properties: Activity and judgment determined more by the external, rather than internal, world. Strong need to communicate with people, high degree of commitment and dedication, promptness, spontaneity, restlessness, highly excitable, identification with other people and the environment. Dominated by feelings (which determine his actions) rather than by rational considerations. High degree of adaptability.

Graphological characteristics: Moderate or gradually expanding left margins, narrow and uneven right margins, moderate to narrow spaces between words and lines, speedy, fluent, and connected writing, rightward slant, highly irregular length, arcades (arc-shaped forms, closed at the top and open at the bottom), ascending alignment, stressed lower zone, leftward direction.

Jung defined four additional components in a person's perception of the world: thinking, sensory perception, emotive feeling, and intuition. Let's look at his division into these types:

Thinking

Thought: Realistic approach to the world, based on logic, objective conclusions, and judgment. Emotionally underdeveloped, every emotional process is rationalized.

Graphological characteristics: Narrow, small, simplified script, connected writing, average and systematic interlinear spacing, emphasized upper zone, original forms, neglected lower zone, mostly leftward slant, abrupt endings.

Sensory Perception

Thought: Understanding of the world based on the senses, weak intuition, but quick, sharp sensory perception (unconscious, but genuine).

Graphological characteristics: Pastiness, smeariness, rightward slant, highly irregular length, broad script, emphasized lower zone, slanted writing, compact script and arrangement.

Sentiment

Thought: understanding and adjustment determined by feelings, reactions based on inner, personal emotional state (which is based only on emotional attitudes, and has no connection with logic or reality).

Graphological characteristics: Developed middle zone, full, swollen, and large letters, arcades or angular arcades, broad script, rightward slant, somewhat pastose (hard, rigid, and messy; simulated) pressure.

Intuition

Thought: Understanding based on a subconscious inner feeling, which perceives and senses future events all of a sudden.

Graphological characteristics: Light, rhythmical, floating, airy pressure and script, disconnected writing, air bridges, very original and simplified script, irregular length, emphasized upper zone, rightward slant, arcades in lower zone.

We can state, however, that these are only the most prominent graphological characteristics, and that each type contains other, less prominent, features as well. Jung himself stated that pure types do not exist; every extrovert contains an introvert, and vice versa. We cannot produce a character analysis based only on type classification. I always teach that graphologists must avoid generalizations; you should always see the unique features of the handwriting sample before you.

William H. Sheldon

William Sheldon compiled an additional typology in 1940. His system is based on the relationship between body and character. He distinguished among three types: the Endomorphous, the Mesomorphous, and the Ectomorphous.

This typology was further developed by Kurtz and Gathy in 1970. They emphasized the fact that the body and temperament are structurally related, even though each does not acknowledge the existence of the other.

	ENDOMORPHOUS	MESOMORPHOUS	ECTOMORPHOUS
PHYSICAL PROPERTIES	round soft	muscular strong athletic	thin delicate fragile
TEMPERAMENT	slow seeking comfort and pleasures sentimental sociable tolerant self-satisfied	active energetic not religious achievement-oriented aggressive courageous seeking danger	sensitive delicate restrained intellectual religiously oriented reserved seeks privacy

PSYCHOPATHOLOGY	changing moods
	including
	excessive depression
	or ecstasy
		deviation
		criminal tendencies
		changing moods
			schizophrenia
			worry and
			  religious neuroses
			suffering from
			  peptic ulcer

Sigmund Freud

Sigmund Freud conceived the theory that human development takes place in stages. Man is driven by the need for pleasure, which is focused in different areas of the body, depending on the given stage of development. Freud named the stages after the areas of the body. The first stage is the oral phase (satisfaction through the lips and the mouth area), the second stage is the anal phase (satisfaction through retainment or release of secretions), the third stage is the phallic stage (satisfaction of the genital region), the fourth stage is the Oedipal phase (sexual feelings for the parent of the opposite sex), the fifth stage is the latency period (latent sexuality in schoolchildren), and the sixth stage is the genital stage (marking the beginning of heterosexual interest). According to Freud, each stage may become fixated. This fixation will determine the individual's type: an oral fixation will produce an oral type, an anal fixation an anal type, and so on.

Erich Fromm

Erich Fromm proposed another system of classification. (He emphasized that his classification is of purely theoretical value, and does not describe any specific individuals.)

Sucking disposition (reception)
This type believes that happiness is to be found in completely external sources, outside himself, and that it is necessary to attain this external source in order to satisfy various needs. It is more important for him to be loved than to love, and he is sensitive to any sign of rejection. When he needs information he tends to look for someone who can provide him with the information, instead of seeking it by himself. His gestures are round and inviting. And he may be religious (i. e., he waits for God to reward him).

Exploitive disposition (taking)
This type also believes that all good things are external, and that it is not possible to create one's own happiness. He believes (in contrast with Type 1) that happiness must be seized. Anything that can be taken from others is better, including love and ideas. This type "milks" other people. His gestures are sharp and aggressive.

Hoarding disposition (preservation)
This type does not believe in receiving things from the external world. He relies on collecting and saving. He tends to be greedy, possessive, extremely neat, and compulsively clean. His gestures are angular and sharp.

Trading disposition (exchange)

This type is manipulative. He sells himself, and changes his loyalties according to his "market value."

In contrast to the four non-productive types I have just described, Fromm stated that there are also productive types. The productive type is characterized by the tendency to realize his potential and latent strengths.

A productive person is capable of using his abilities wisely in order to realize his potential. He has to be free and independent, without any external control on his powers. We must distinguish between productivity and creativity, especially of the artistic kind. When we say "creativity," we mean the fulfilling of a person's potential. Although most artists are creative, not all are productive. It is possible to produce routinely, for example, by copying a figure mechanically, like a camera, without fulfilling yourself or making full use of your potential. The opposite is also true – you can be creative, but without the ability to transmit any message.

It is important for you to see these different properties quantitavely; that is, someone may possess a certain quality in varying degrees. In reality, people also possess mixtures of these dispositions, and not the pure dispositions we have described here.

Israel Odem

We cannot conclude this chapter on personality without mentioning the Israeli graphologist Israel Odem, who created an innovative typology in his book *Handwriting and Personality*. Odem is the first graphologist to have developed a theory of "potentials" based solely on handwriting, without relying on psychological classification systems, as his predecessors had done. The advantage of this theory is that it is not based on any abstract typology, but rather on graphological facts alone. It springs from within a person's handwriting, and does not impose on handwriting the abstract criteria developed by psychologists. Odem realized that handwriting cannot be singled out from a person's general functional system, just as a person's character cannot be examined in a purely quantitative manner. After all, we are dealing with dynamic human beings, and not with cold statistics.

But, as Otto Jung said, "Human handwriting cannot be understood as a whole." We must begin by examining details, followed by the construction of syndromes and then larger units of the personality. We must begin with the measurement and examination of individual signs through an analytical process. Together with a clearly scientific examination, this will enable us to create an artistic-intuitive synthesis describing the whole person.

In his book, Odem developed a method for firmly establishing the "guiding idea," which before Odem had only been subjective and intuitive. He took all 32 "families" of movement, shape, and organization, and discovered homogenous signs, which occur in coordination with each other.

Odem also claimed, justifiably, that we can find a combination of potentials in each person. The graphologist must understand the relative strength of the components of this combination, and the manner in which they join together. Finally, Odem singled out nine potentials relating to the slant of the writing, the homogeneity of the script, and the manner in which the graphological signs are integrated into the overall arrangement and form.

Помните, любите, изучайте Ильича, нашего учителя, нашего вождя. Боритесь и побеждайте врагов, внутренних и внешних, — по Ильичу.

Стройте новую жизнь, новый быт, новую культуру — по Ильичу. Никогда не отказывайтесь от малого в работе, ибо из малого строится великое, — в этом один из <u>важных заветов Ильича</u>

Здравствуй, мой воробушек! Пишу и помню. За работу спасибо. Только ради труда, голубчик, больше не присылай мне работы.

Если тебе так приятно в Кремль, можешь остаться в Кремле не велеть.

Целую крепко. 7/VII 38. Твой папка.

Joseph Stalin I

Joseph Stalin II

Changes in Personality and Handwriting

Your handwriting is as dynamic as your personality. Humans change constantly, and we frequently discover new elements of a person's character, which come into existence within hours, or even seconds. Guilt feelings are a good example. We all suffer on occasion from a bad conscience, and this feeling will be reflected in our handwriting at the time, while it will be absent at other times. Other changes, such as illness, depression, or enthusiasm, are also revealed in our handwriting.

Let's look at a few examples of radical changes in people's handwriting. Our first two samples are of the handwriting of Joseph Stalin, whose personality I once described on my radio show as that of a priest turned murderer.

You can see in sample I that the stroke is soft, smooth, and open towards others. The pressure is weak, the script is small, and seems to be shy and sensitive.

You can immediately spot the changes in sample II, written when Stalin was already a dictator, with rivers of blood on his hands. The writing is hard, rigid, and messy (pastose, in graphological terminology). It contains stains and aggressive lines, especially in the lower part of this sample. Angular and rigid handwriting may indicate an evil disposition and cruelty. If you look at the vertical line separating day from month, you will notice that it resembles the trunk of an "amputated" oak tree (see chapter on pressure).

стекло

в первый день

запомни 26/VI-81

Felix I

You can see changes in size, speed, and pressure in Felix's handwriting. He was very angry when he wrote the first sample, while he was in a more normal state of mind when he wrote the second sample. You can notice that he even crossed out mistakes differently in the two samples: his cancelling strokes in the first sample are angry, very aggressive, sharp, and extreme.

Felix II

Joan's handwriting contains the most substantial differences in the script of the same person that I have ever come across. Joan has spent a lot of time in mental institutions, and her personality has undergone radical changes. Look at these four handwriting examples of Joan's. They are so different, with almost no shared features, that without being told you would not know that they were written by the same person.

Where do you go from there?
let's hope get married (lord,
what a gold mine — a 4f! — I'm
purplish greenish reddish with
grey) But what if you don't?

Joan   I

The trouble is I blame myself
am full of guilt and remorse
for not being able to manage
my life without depending on
him so much.. It The next step

Joan   II

week so I can get
all my business
attended to soon.
 I have to pay my
rent and bills before
I can retire to the
hospital.

Joan III

anything.
 Could you
find out where
they are? I have
written Bob but he
doesn't want

I guess I am
hopelessly insane.
All I can do
is worry about

Joan IV

În primul rând vreau să-ți urez să
reușești în să ai succes în carieră și să
devii faimoasă în lumea întreagă
Ai muncit greu în tot ce ai obținut la
ora actuală este numai datorită ție
voinței tale, talentului tău și inteligenței

Simona I

Bicicleta mea este cumpărată
dela curtea regală Tatăl meu mi-a
cumpărat-o a aparținut unei prințese

Simona II

SIMONA
LAZAROVICI

Simona III

We can see a completely different type of change in Simona's handwriting. The first sample is written in her regular, spontaneous handwriting. It is rather fast and connected in a harmonious manner. The pressure is continuous, and her writing is fluent, without interruptions.

The second sample was written when Simona was under the influence of hypnosis, after she had been told "you are now 15 years old." Her writing has become much slower, the pressure is stronger, the direction more upright, and the lines go up, as opposed to the straight alignment in the first sample. The script is bigger, and the punctuation signs are clumsy and large. It took Simona much more time to write these three lines than the entire first page, which was not written under hypnosis.

In the third example, the hypnotist sent Simona back to the age of six when she only knew how to print her name.

We see from this experiment that handwriting may be influenced by conscious and unconscious changes occuring in the brain.

On the other hand, the handwriting of a completely bilingual person will contain the same characteristic features, in both languages. David speaks both English and Hebrew. If you examine David's handwriting samples, you will be able to locate matching features in both the English and Hebrew samples. (Remember, Hebrew is written from right to left.) Look at the margins, the size of the spaces between words, and even the structure of garlands in the lower zone – all these elements are almost identical.

אני חושב את הדברים האלה כמו שיש לי אותן

פולים צודקים ואני יש בקצת כתב יד-י אתון

וכו'. אפשר להם ללמדים

The more I speak with you about the whole subject of the training, the more clear I become about the fact that this itself is

David

Here is another sample of David's handwriting. This sample is from another period in his life, and his script is smaller. Once again, you can find a great deal of similarity between the English and Hebrew samples, in the arrangement on the page, size, forms, and other features. We can conclude from this that changes occur in both languages in the same manner.

David

Analyzing Your Handwriting

Now that we've studied the history of graphology, and learned some of the basic concepts of this science, you can start analyzing your own handwriting. Here are a few basic instructions.

Tools of the Trade:
pen – you have to write with a ball point pen, and it must write properly. It is important that your pen does not leak, and that there aren't any problems with the point (sticking, ink stoppage, etc).
table – you have to write in a comfortable position (sitting down!), on a solid table with a smooth surface.
paper – use large sheets of smooth paper. Do not use absorbent paper, nor ruled paper.

All of these tools should function well, in order to avoid distortions in your handwriting and its analysis. Later on, you will need additional tools: a transparent ruler, a protractor, a magnifying glass, and lots of patience.

Procedure:
Write at least 20 lines, preferably more. Your writing should be spontaneous, which means that you should not copy from a book or write what someone dictates to you. When you take dictation, the auditory, visual, and writing centers in your brain are activated by other stimuli. As a result, other brain functions, such as thinking and the ability to concentrate, are not fully active. Your writing becomes synthetic, rather than natural,

preventing the graphologist from receiving important information. The same is true of copying a text. In addition to what happens during dictation, when you copy you have to stop from time to time to look at the text which you are copying. A graphologist may interpret these interruptions as disturbances in your concentration. You must remember not to copy, and not to ask other people to dictate to you, in order to avoid such distortions.

It is important to be relaxed and comfortable while writing, so you should not write while standing or travelling, nor should you write on your lap. If you write in these positions, your writing will be different.

Write in the language which you are most familiar with, and which you usually use. It is impossible to analyze your handwriting if you do not write in an orderly manner, or if you write in an unfamiliar language. Your writing must be fluent and spontaneous without pauses between letters. You pause between letters when you are unsure of the script and style (such as immigrants writing in their newly-acquired language).

Your writing should be normal. Do not try to write "perfect" letters, and do not try to print letters as if your sample were a book.

Finished?

You can also look for old samples of your handwriting, and collect them as well. You can use old letters. Lines are not that important for now, so the page does not have to be unruled. But don't choose short notes or shopping lists.

At a later stage, when you examine other people's handwriting, you will have to ask for additional information, such as sex, age, and education.

You will need all these facts in order to produce an accurate graphological analysis. Carelessness will produce poor results. Be accurate, and you won't be disappointed!

I want to emphasize that your reading this book will not turn you into a graphologist.

This book will enrich your knowledge on the subject and teach you a few professional secrets, but you should not think that you are a professional graphologist or present yourself as a graphologist to others. Doing so may cause great harm to the people whose handwriting you analyze or to the people who ask you to prepare an analysis.

I deliberately did not include in this book all the graphological information I possess; not because I want to conceal information, but because a little knowledge can be dangerous. Even after many years of study, with the experience of thousands of analyses, I still am very cautious, and check and recheck myself before stating my professional opinion.

I rely on you to acknowledge your lack of expertise, and hope that this book will stimulate you to continue your study of graphology.

Aquarious

It is a beautiful day today
I'm happy I happened to
come this way as I live in

the opposite direction

Lisa

I have called twice about the
furniture but neither call has
produced results. I am curious
about what the guarantee

Martha

Rules of Handwriting Analysis

Let's take a look at two handwriting samples, while we learn some of the basic rules of handwriting analysis. You can see that these two samples share a number of identical characteristics: the script is large, and the inflated upper zone is especially prominent. Both samples have exaggerated swellings in the upper half of the letters.

In the sample of Martha's handwriting, you can see that the letters "Y," "H," and "T" are very full, out of all proportion to the rest of the writing. The letters "Y" and "H" are also large and inflated in Lisa's handwriting. If you compare the word "I" in Martha's writing with "I" in Lisa's handwriting, you will find that the letters "I" are very similar. But take a closer look. You can see that Lisa's handwriting is different. The lower part of the same letter "I" looks as bulging as the upper part, while in the sample of Martha's handwriting, the swelling is bigger in the upper zone.

You will find many differences in the other graphological features of the two samples. Martha's writing seems to be more stable and systematic, while Lisa's handwriting shows much less coherence and firmness. You can learn from this exercise that even identical signs must be analyzed within the full context of the handwriting, since the same sign may be interpreted differently in different contexts, regarding the writing sample as an organic unit. Martha is a woman with a great deal of imagiation and originality; she also is very superficial. Lisa, on the other hand, is a tense, confused, hysterical, and unstable woman.

As you gain more experience, you will learn to analyze handwriting with more precision. As you do so, you must always remember these five basic rules of graphology.

Rule One

Every sign you see may have multiple meanings.

You should not reach hasty conclusions. Carefully examine each sign, both on its own as well as within the broader context of the entire handwriting sample. Check yourself several times, employing different perspectives, before you describe any quality of the writer's character.

Rule Two

Not all of the characteristics appearing in the same column of a table are suitable for a specific person.

Each of the following chapters in this book concludes with one or more tables, with a list of properties under each sign. All of these properties cannot possibly be possessed by a single person, and we must consider a number of additional factors. In most cases, you will select between two and five of the most characteristic features. In columns containing a larger number of features, you may find nine or ten which are relevant, but this is a very remote possibility.

At times, you will find that a handwriting sample contains two graphological characteristics, which appear in the same table in two different columns. In such a case, the character features of the writer are to be found in the two columns.

Rule Three

The degree of prominence of a sign corresponds to the number of its character features.

I. e., the more prominent a sign is, the more character features will be associated with it.

As you continue to analyze your handwriting, you will find that most of its graphological characteristics will appear over and over again.

Rule Four

The more exaggerated a graphological sign, the more character features may be selected from the bottom of a column.

Rule Five

The more a graphological sign is repeated, the more dominant are its corresponding character features, and vice versa – a sign which appears only once may be disregarded.

Margins

Margins are the white areas which remain empty as we write on a sheet of paper. We usually leave margins in the upper and lower parts of the sheet, as well as on both the left and right sides of the paper.

The margins form a frame for the written text, and express limitations: you are willing to write from here (the starting margin) to here (the ending margin), and no more.

You are taught to leave margins from the time you start learning how to write. Even today, some teachers still instruct their pupils, "Put two fingers on the left side of the page and start writing after them." In other words, they stipulate uniform margins. This uniformity changes for most people as they mature and their personal qualities become crystallized. They acquire different margins, which reflect their personality and state of mind.

The width of the left margin is determined when you first put your pen on the paper, namely as you write the first letter on the page. This first touch of the pen on the paper is known as an "entrance." You "entered" the page and created a point marking the space you have left, the top and left margins. This point may be anywhere in the upper left quadrant of the page. You have left the first "calling card" for the graphologist, which, together with other "calling cards," enables him to examine your behavior from the moment of your entrance to the moment you leave. We can compare this entry to your entering a house: if you establish immediate contact with the people present, and carry on a lively flow of conversation – your margins will be narrower; if you wait on the doorstep, and hesitate – your margins will be wider.

Hiermit nochmals eine Probe
meiner Handschrift.
Vielleicht habe ich heute eine
andere Laune.

15. 11. 77.

Freida

You can see that there is a connection between the arrangement of your writing on the page and your attitude towards other people. We can also learn from this about your relationship with the person to whom the page is addressed.

The margins on your shopping list and on short notes you write for yourself or your roommate are different from the margins on a letter to your congressman or on a letter applying for a job. As soon as you begin writing, you leave an empty, white space, which reveals your conscious or unconscious attitude to your past. The exact spot where you begin writing is the present. The closer you come to the right side of the page, the closer you come to other people and to your future (again, as they are captured in your conscious and unconscious mind). Your progress forward on the page symbolizes your looking ahead into the future.

The arrangement of the margins may tell us something about the writer's aesthetic sense: a good arrangement of the page, with even margins on all four sides (top, bottom, left, and right) indicates a highly developed sense of beauty.

We can see this in our first sample. It was written by Freida, a woman artist, who organized the page like a painting: the writing is in the center of the page surrounded by a white frame.

The way we arrange the page indicates our economical attitudes. It is only logical that a thrifty person would fill the page from beginning to end, without wasting a single inch of writing space, sometimes even filling in the margins. The wasteful/extravagant type, on the other hand, does not try to save on paper. He starts writing in the middle of the page, moving on to a new sheet of paper after a few lines.

A pitfall awaits you here if you're not careful. As I have already stated, an isolated graphological sign is almost meaningless. If you find that there are no other indications of stinginess besides the absence of margins, it is essential (as in any other case) that you determine the writer's mother tongue. In some countries, such as in South America, people are taught to write without any margins at all. In such a case, the lack of margins obviously does not have the same meaning as it does for a writer who learned to leave a margin of two fingers wide.

It is almost impossible to maintain straight, book-like margins. It is easier to keep the left margin even, since you keep returning to the same place with your pen. The right margin is harder to keep straight; even typewriters are equipped with a special signal to alert the typist that the end of the line is near. This difficulty exists due to the fact that each word contains a different number of letters, and it is not easy for the writer to anticipate and control their length. When you want to measure the right margin, you must check whether the word on the next line, including the space, could have been fitted into the previous line; if so, we call this a "crooked" margin.

Let's look at the handwriting of two Presidents, George Washington and Abraham Lincoln, before we examine the handwriting of other people in more detail. The margins in Lincoln's handwriting are particularly even, which usually indicates stability, self-control, concern with one's appearance, strict discipline, and the ability to function well within a clearly defined framework. You can see that the manner of arrangement and margin formation in George Washington's handwriting are almost identical with those in Lincoln's writing.

Abraham Lincoln

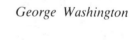

George Washington

Now look at these two samples. The first feature you may notice is that both writers formed a straight left margin. Although both writers share this feature, their characters are completely different. Harold's rows are overlapping. This indicates a feeling of suffocation: the script is jammed, there are no spaces left, we can feel the very lack of air. David, on the other hand, leaves wide spaces between the rows, and the entire atmosphere in this second sample is different.

Harold's extremely straight left margins are obsessive. He is afraid, and he struggles against a loss of control, which reveals his inner conflicts. David deliberately maintains straight margins. Margins are a way of coping within a framework; he wants to adapt himself to his environment. There is also evidence of an organizational skill.

Harold

David

Dird —

Here is a sample of

my handwriting. See

See what you will.

Marc

CARTE POSTALE

Communication—Correspondance   Address—Adresse

Дарю свою фотографию
семье Гринглаз от Муси
Кибрик с совместной
жизни во время
Эмиграции

Southempton 18/III – 24

Musia

In Marc's handwriting you will find wide margins (both left and right). The arrangement on the page makes the sample look more like a poem than a letter. Our tables indicate that a wide left margin suggests an aesthetic sense, and that a very wide right margin is a sign of a poetic soul. In actuality, Marc is an interesting combination of a psychologist, artist, poet, and… a graphologist. The drawing surrounding his writing shows his artistic talent, and the arrangement of the page reveals his tendency to write poetry. His handwriting itself will reveal the rest of his character, as you will learn for yourself.

Musia's handwriting has concave margins. Our table indicates infantility, which characterizes his handwriting as a whole. It looks very childish and undeveloped, graphologically speaking. Even if you can't read Russian, you can clearly see that this sample is modelled on the pattern taught in school. It is written slowly, with no momentum and no originality.

In Alice's handwriting you can easily see a diminishing left margin and a very wide and disappearing right margin. You will find the following properties in the table for a diminishing left margin: inhibitions, severe self-criticism, fear of failure. And for very wide right margins: strong sense of responsibility, fear of failure, excessive caution. Under diminishing margins, you'll find slow progress and caution.

we are having a most
enjoyable trip. we always
love being in Israel. This
has been a very interesting
experience this morning being
here with these lovely ladies
and learning something more
about myself and handwriting
analysis. I am extremely tired
at this moment especially getting
over a cold and since I am passed
60 years of age I can't complain.

Alice

Jennifer's handwriting has wide, slightly crooked margins. From the list of character features for wide margins, we may select politeness, ability to perform, aesthetic sense, and running away from memories. The crooked margin list includes love of adventure and moodiness. I have chosen these traits because they will be revealed by a comprehensive analysis of Jennifer's handwriting. I have excluded other qualities mentioned in the lists because they are not part of her overall personality.

Now is the time for all good men to come to
the aid of the party. Happy Birthday to you,
you belong in the zoo, with the elephants
and the donkeys happy birthday to you.
Once I was happy but now I'm forlorn,
like an old coat that is tattered and
torn, left in this wide world to weep

Jennifer

Our next handwriting sample was written by Orna Porat, a famous Israeli actress. Porat was born as a Christian, in Germany, and later converted to Judaism. We can see that she left a wide left margin, telling us of a painful past. Her tendency to write on the margin reveals her responsible attitude towards the past: she is aware of her past, but not bothered by it. This can also reveal a tendency to fill in spaces, like standing on a stage, and chattiness.

Orna Porat

收到你十二月十日的來信、內有相片六張，聖誕咭一張、及信一封；為什麼我如數數給你知，因為信完全能拆開，我恐怕你們附寄什麽貴重東西夾在其中寄來，被人偷去。故下次來信請告知有否什麽東西遺漏。故最請你們以後寄什麽貴重東西寄掛號，以免損失。

我們去聖誕前已寄出兩張支票，一張給你（代我替四姊買嬰兒用品給四姊的新女兒，並代恭祝他）另一張是寄給月珍是奉還所欠的。下次來信請告知你們收到否：

我們已找到工作，Jacob與我月得那舊鄰居中國女子介紹，在他工作在這裏的希伯來大學之便，得一份抄寫、打字及翻譯工作；而我另得一份医院工作，每星期工作五天，那是一間新医院，開始剛年半，而有趣的是那是一間宗教甚嚴的医院。我不能返回舊時工作過的那間醫院工作，因他們知我不會長做；而這次我面試當然不告訴他們我只幫時性工作，否則他們不會聘請我的。故此，新的一年稍有一點新希望，因你不會明白這裏東西貴的程度，只是食物要花你不少錢，若我們不能工作，沒有收入，試想怎能應付呢！因幸然使我們有薪金，交租、一切水電煤氣費、去買食物外，便無所餘，而去香港，這樣情況下最低限度能剩到一些錢，買到一些東西，在這裏，簡直是妄想。若順利的話，能得到經濟幫助成功到美國完成Jacob的手術，這次我医院工作可能是子長久。促你有很重的路要走、其中經歷真是子能筆墨能形容的。再者，上述那份抄寫工作我予以在家中做。

Natalie I

These two samples, in different languages, were both written by the same person, Natalie. The left margins in both samples are straight and well-organized. We learn from this phenomena that features do not change from the point of view of the graphologist, even when someone writes in more than one language.

REACTION AND BELIEF

APTITUDE AND BEHAVIOUR

(A) MEASURE OF APTITUDE

(B) APTITUDE TEST

(C) EXTREMITY OF APTITUDE

(D) DIFFERENTIAL OF MOB APTITUDE

PROFESSIONAL

(A) JOB SATISFACTION

(1) REWARD

Natalie II

אתך בכל פעם מברר לי על זה וכן את אאר לעצמי

כך (Acknowledgement) . . אין אומר על כל מקרה לי

"וכבד של ה-Acknowledgement זאת היא . יותר אאלנים אתך

אין בתם את בדברים האלה על ד גם אני וכם

פואם אותם ואני פולה ד קבל ברב-ד בזה אתן

וכן . אלכם סם בתב לאאלכי

אלכלי סם בתב לאאלכי

The more I speak with you about the whole

subject of the training, the more clear I

become about the fact that this itself is

something I must "get off"! Sharing my

experiences and thoughts with you is   *David*

Our next two samples were also writtten by one person, writing in two languages. David wrote the top sample in Hebrew, and the bottom sample in English. I want to point out here that since Hebrew is written from right to left, the right margin in Hebrew corresponds to the left margin in English (and other languages written in Roman characters), and the left margin in Hebrew corresponds to the right margin in English. If you examine David's two samples, you will notice that the left margin in the English sample is completely identical with the right margin in his Hebrew sample.

In Marie's sample we see a right margin narrowing towards the end. You can clearly see that the writer proceeds step by step. Our character's features list shows that Marie's handwriting reveals increased caution, and that her personal potential is gradually developing.

à l'ofital. 10. ans - fai -

j'aime ma famille et surtout -

un fils quit est a l'armie -

j'ai un marie qui est tes

jalouse. moi jaire rien la vie

je suis une bonne maman .

moi il me manque quelques chose

dans ma vie - je suis tès

Marie

Of course there is not everything to write with, but I
shall compensate. A pen a
pencil, a quill a felt tip
pen and any thing else
you can think of.

Edna

Edna's sample has widening left margins and a right margin widening towards the end. According to the widening left margin table, Edna's outstanding traits are openness, honesty, attempts to be sociable, naturalness, creativity, and love of life. The table for wide right margins includes responsibility for one's actions, stopping and observing situations, independence, fear of failure, inhibitions due to past disappointments, and fears. If we base our analysis on the traits revealed by margins, we are faced with a seeming contradiction: openness and allied traits, on the one hand, and inhibitions, on the other. We can resolve this seeming contradiction by conducting an in-depth analysis of all the other features of Edna's writing. We would learn that, in spite of her indicated spontaneity, Edna keeps herself in check, in order to avoid further disappointments. Increased caution and less spontaneity is indicated.

You have learned from these examples that the different properties in the appropriate tables overlap, complement, and even contradict each other. In the beginning, you may have to copy all the character features from the entire table(s). Only at later stages will you be able to sort out the properties which appear only once. But, gradually, if you develop the right perception of handwriting and the atmosphere it generates, you will be able to choose only those qualities which are relevant to the specific person being analyzed.

Left Margin

Very Wide

_____ possibility of mental disorder
_____ escape from memories due
_____ to a painful past
_____ seeks to approach others,
_____ and escape from oneself
_____ urge to prove oneself
_____ demanding
_____ haughtiness
_____ aloofness
conceit
repression

Wide

_____ politeness, formality
_____ demonstrativeness
_____ aesthetic sense
_____ love of luxury
_____ extravagance
_____ feeling of deprivation
_____ escape from memories
_____ due to a painful past
_____ pretense of happiness and
 content with one's lot

Medium, even

_____ formality
_____ care for appearance
_____ pleasantness
_____ sense of order
_____ talent to organize
_____ meticulousness
_____ ability to assess and evaluate
_____ inner discipline
_____ perseverance
_____ stability
self-control

Narrow, even

_____ balanced judgment
_____ inner discipline
_____ self-criticism
_____ cautious planning
_____ ability to resist
_____ strictness
_____ talent to organize
_____ adjustment to frameworks
_____ economy
conservativeness
selfishness

Missing margin

_____ excessive self-confidence
_____ defensive
_____ authoritarian
_____ suspicion
_____ mentally suppressed
_____ selfishness
_____ indifference
_____ arrogance
_____ strong materialism
stinginess
talkativeness

Wavy margin

_____ insecurity
_____ inner struggle, hesitation
_____ defensive (feels attacked)
_____ moodiness
_____ disturbances in concentration
_____ lack of independence
_____ impressionability
_____ adventurous imagination
_____ lack of emotional stability
alternations between elation
 and depression

Widening margin
need for self-expression
recovered self-confidence
openness
sincerity
yearning for social contact
naturalness
creativity
love of life
ambition
overcoming suspicions
impulsiveness
impatience
curiosity
hot-tempered
aggresiveness

Narrowing margin
inhibitions
excessive self-criticism
concealed plans
guilt feelings
bad conscience
self-torment
fear of failure
flight from reality
egocentricity
stinginess
hesitancy

Irregular, widening
restraint
suppressed desires
dissatisfaction with oneself
fear of commitment
inhibitions
feeling of being cheated

Irregular, narrrowing
indecision
self-torment
satirical approach to life
bitterness
stubbornness due to disappointment
incapability of achieving more,
ambition exceeds realization

Concave
impulses precede thought
alternating between elation
and depression
suppressed impulsiveness
forced spontaneity
childishness

Convex
thought precedes impulses
delayed or gradual growing enthusiasm
fear of action

Right Margin

Very wide
strong sense of responsibility
stops to check situations
fear of failure, excessive caution
desire for independence
poetic soul
keeps a distance
indecision
hesitation
disappointment
unforgiving (bearing a grudge)
selfishness
despair at times

Medium, relatively even
coolness
suspicion
thriftiness
inhibitions
security wall around oneself
keeping distance
hard to approach
fear of failure
pretensions

Narrow, relatively even
feeling of self-inspection
caution
balanced judgment
physical self-control

Narrow, uneven
courage
activism
daring to the point of carelessness
sociability
impulsiveness
inability to keep one's distance
inconsideration

Wavy
inventiveness
originality, dislike
 of the conventional
restlessness
urge to travel
weak-willed
lack of perseverance
feeling of disadvantage
fear of repeating failures
cultivating of illusions
demonstrative independence
irresponsibility

Missing margin
alertness
reliance on oneself
enthusiasm
courage
excitability
talkativeness
fast thinking
fast talking
fast acting – quick writer
stinginess – slow writer
inconsideration

Widening margin

fearfulness
disappointment
demanding
feeling of inferiority
self-accusation
selfishness

Irregular

suspicion
accusing attitude towards others
insecurity
sarcasm
cynicism
self-justification
difficulty in admitting mistakes

Narrowing

slow progress
caution
desire to correct distortions
need for achievement
gradual development
 of individual potential

Irregular breaks into margin

inconsideration
aggressiveness
impulsiveness caused by shyness

Top and Bottom Margins

Top and bottom margins are less important than the left and right ones, although they do have some significance of their own. The top margin reflects your entry into the page. Just as in the case of the left margin, the exact point of entry, i. e. the space you leave behind, has meaning. A polite writer will leave a moderate space of one or two lines; a spontaneous or impertinent writer will start at the very top of the page, without leaving any space at all. An arrogant writer will leave a very wide margin (several lines); it takes him some time before he starts writing.

The bottom margin represents the departure from the page. When the writer has nothing to say, you can predict that the bottom margin will be wide. Well-organized people will leave a small margin, and talkative people will leave no bottom margin at all.

Top Margin

Wide
self-confidence
formality
politeness
difficulty in initiating conversations
respect for fellow men
balanced judgment
arrogance
aloofness
pretentiousness
contemptuous view of the world
snobbishness
pretensions

Narrow
matter-of-fact approach to life
modesty
sense of proportion
narrowmindedness
conventionality
anxiety
pettiness

Missing
naturalness
direct approach to the world
sincerity
spontaneity
talkativeness
impoliteness
disregard for people
crudity

Bottom Margin

Large
ability to get
  to the heart of matters
ability to summarize
lack of confidence
mental distress
feeling of deprivation
laziness

Small
balanced judgment
ability to plan ahead
good organizing ability
economy

Missing
urgency of purpose
tension
uninhibited
talkativeness
adventurous
inconsideration
stinginess

Interlinear Spacing

A certain amount of empty space is usually left between lines of handwriting; it is called "interlinear spacing" in graphological terminology. Obviously, you can analyze spacing only when your sample has been written on a blank, unruled sheet of paper. There are no fixed rules governing the size of interlinear spacing. The same space which may seem small to you in large handwriting may seem big in small handwriting.

Some graphologists consider the height of the middle zone, that is, the height of the letters "c," "e," "o," and "r" as the clear interlinear space. A space which is smaller than the height of these letters will be perceived as being narrow, while a larger space will be considered to be wide. In my opinion, a clear space is one where the lower loops of letters such as "g" and "y" almost touch the upper loops of letters such as "l," "k," and "f." The space is wide if another line can be added between the existing ones, and it is narrow if there is any contact between the descending letters of one line and the ascending letters of the next line. The writing becomes confused when the space is so narrow that the letters actually intermingle, disregarding the line which was previously written.

Interlinear spacing may reveal information on the intellectual and social aspects of your personality. On the intellectual aspect, the spaces between the lines show clarity, objectivity, organizational ability, and the ability to concentrate. Socially, spacing shows your ability for good social relations, attitude towards society and your fellow human beings, and your manners.

When the interlinear spacing is exaggeratedly wide, and there are also wide spaces between words, you receive the impression that each word is an island of its own. An only child, or someone who behaves as if he were, will leave exaggerated spaces. His judgment ceases to be objective, and becomes demanding. Other writers who leave large spaces between lines suffer from concentration problems (they advance slowly from one word to the next and from one line to the next, and there is no immediate continuity between lines).

120

You can easily see that the interlinear spaces in James' handwriting are exaggerated. Look at your chart: you will find properties such as a lack of realism and demandingness. If you look further in the chart, you will also find isolation, passivity, lack of communication with others, and other traits. The next chart you must look at refers to word interspaces: there is a direct connection between social contacts and the spaces between lines and between words. A lonely person such as James, who is isolated and antisocial, will leave wide spaces between both lines and words. It is not likely that an antisocial person will only leave wide spaces between the lines. You should know, of course, that you will have to prove your diagnosis on the basis of additional charts and features, as well.

James

Jenny's handwriting has exaggerated interlinear spacing. Look at the table: the first character trait listed is a lack of realism. This trait is supported by the peculiar bubbles in Jenny's script, which also indicate that the writer lives in a fantasy world, with an unrealistic approach to the real world. She writes in a careless manner; this shows us that Jenny does not care very much about her relations with other people. We all know that writing is an extremely important means of communication, second in importance only to speech. Careless handwriting can hardly contribute to better interpersonal communication.

Hoy es martes y estoy en una conferencia acerca de Grafología. Dejé en eso a los chicos con Ani y me costó bastante dado que el piola que se fui lo pueda. Lo supuesto que le deje que si que acepta ba que fuera se desprendiera del

Jenny

122

Paulette's handwriting has clear spaces between the lines, which tend to become narrower. She is a cautious planner, systematic, and has an aesthetic sense.

Chère Madame

Nous avons bien reçu votre lettre et le chèque de 200 L.I. inclus. Nous vous réservons donc une chambre du 10 au 17 février, et une autre pour votre secrétaire du 13 au 17 février. Si vous préférez être ensemble, ce sera possible aussi. A très bientôt donc.

Paulette

As you can see from his handwriting, Harold has a completely different personality. He suffers from such a severe feeling of mental suffocation that he had to be hospitalized at the time he wrote this sample.

Harold

I have only just begun. This piece of paper is very small. I prefer to write on large sheets of paper. Empty space open free unending I've enjoyed talking to you. Well, this is it.

Pat

In Pat's handwriting, the spaces between the lines are extremely narrow, so much so that the text is unclear and difficult to read. You feel a sense of suffocation and a lack of objectivity. It seems that Pat does not mind that her writing is illegible. You can assume from this that she is also indifferent to the fact that other people cannot understand her.

The interlinear spaces in Randy's handwriting are very narrow, and become narrower as the text progresses. The space between the last two lines is much smaller than the space between the first two lines. It is true that the gradual narrowing is due to Randy's realization that he is approaching the end of the page, indicating bad planning. This change also indicates childlike quality, lack of clarity, lack of objectivity, and most likely bad vision.

In Francine's handwriting, you will find very narrow spaces between the lines, to the point of illegibility. The script is rigid, and you can easily spot the unclear spacing, with letters written on top of others. Our tables indicate that Francine is subjective, with unclear judgment, inflexible, and lacking clarity.

Your voice is the most beautiful in all the world. When you ask me what a word means I _melt_. All the days I think of you.

If I am not for myself, who will be for me; if I am only for myself, what am I? and if not now, when?

To me this means the stronger I become the more people I can help and if we do not do something immediately we may never get the opportunity to do it.

Kips

Jumper in mid-air at Intervale Ski Jump
III Winter Olympic Games, Lake Placid, 1932

Randy

As I told you I departured to the seaside at the first time to spend there two great months of my life.

You know the life on the sea coast is different from that one in Bucharest. It's something strange "the Time" began another dimension, the events come more in number and of course the news too.

A day there is a different kind of day. It is more lived.

Francine

Interlinear Spacing

	Exaggerated space	Clear space	Narrowing towards end of page
SOCIAL	*lack of realism* *demanding* *loneliness* *passivity* *isolation* *spoiled* *possibly an only child* *arrogance* *aloofness* *wastefulness*	*politeness* *tact* *cool relations* *with other people* *lack of spontaneity*	*excessive talkativeness* *loss of self-control*
INTELLECTUAL	*disturbed concentration* *lack of objectivity* *indifference* *undisciplined thinker* *difficulty in connecting* *different things* *very few associations*	*balanced judgment* *sense of proportion* *matter-of-factness* *logic* *clear thinking* *ability to summarize* *ability to concentrate* *ability to evaluate* *good organizational skills* *good managerial skills* *analytic thinking* *objectivity* *clarity*	*loss of clarity*

Narrow	Widening towards end of page	Very narrow
warmth	*uncontrolled instincts*	*stubbornness*
sincerity		*indifference to being*
naturalness		*understood by others*
spontaneity		*insincerity*
friendliness		*suppression*
devotion		*camouflage*
involvement		*stinginess*
lack of reserve		*childishness (infantilism)*
need to communicate		
pathos		
life of the present		
thoroughness	*weakening of mental*	*lack of objectivity*
intellectual preference to be active	*and/or physical stability*	*(may be shortsighted)*
subjectivity		
lack of clear judgment		
dogmatism		
lack of clarity		
difficulty in expressing oneself		
confusion		

Spaces between Words

Writing consists of a system of letters which are divided by spaces between lines and between words. Without these spaces, your handwriting would be incomprehensible. The two types of spacing are closely related, since both have very similar properties.

The normal space between two words is the size of 1½ – 2 round letters. As we learned in the previous chapter on interlinear spacing, spacing between words can tell us something about the manner in which you think and about your social behavior.

The space you leave between two words reveals your attitude towards your fellow human beings. The beginning of the word is a reflection of yourself, and the conclusion of the word reflects your attitude towards others. (I will discuss this point at length in the chapter regarding changes the word, represents the "me," while its end reflects

your attitude to "you." The space between the words teaches us about your relationship with other people.

You will find very narrow, almost nonexistent spaces between the words in Harold's handwriting (which we already examined in the chapter discussing margins). We learn from this feature that he has an acute need for social contact, so much so that he has lost all control over his ties with other people. He approaches other people indiscriminately and, actually, with no regard for them. The interlinear spacing in his handwriting also is very narrow, making the writing almost illegible. Harold writes without giving other people a chance to understand him. This obviously reveals a severe mental disturbance. It is quite surprising, on the other hand, to see such straight and neat margins. In contrast with the stark picture presented by the other types of spacing, the margins appear to be compulsive and not suited to the form of the text.

Let's look at the Hebrew handwriting of Uri Avneri, an Israeli journalist and former member of the Israeli parliament, the Knesset. He writes with normal spaces, which shows us that he has a balanced social attitude, he chooses his friends, does not form contacts easily with everyone, nor does he keep his distance in an exaggerated manner. As for his intellectual qualities, we can conclude (together with other graphological signs) that he is a clear thinker, has a sense of order, organizational ability, a sense of proportion, and speedy comprehension, and is logical and possesses analytical ability.

Uri Avneri

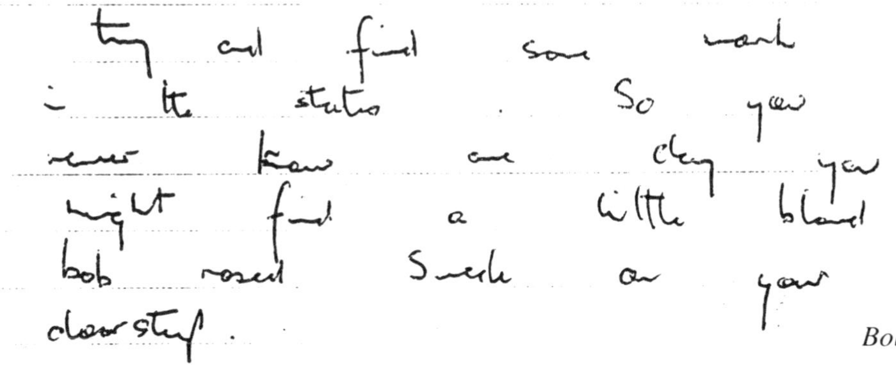

Here, here are cool green bowers.

[handwritten sample, mostly illegible]

try and find some work
in the states. So you
never know one day you
might find a little blond
bob rosed Suck on your
door step.

Bobby

Bobby writes with very wide spaces between words in this sample.

Juanita, on the other hand, has narrow spaces between the words in her handwriting.

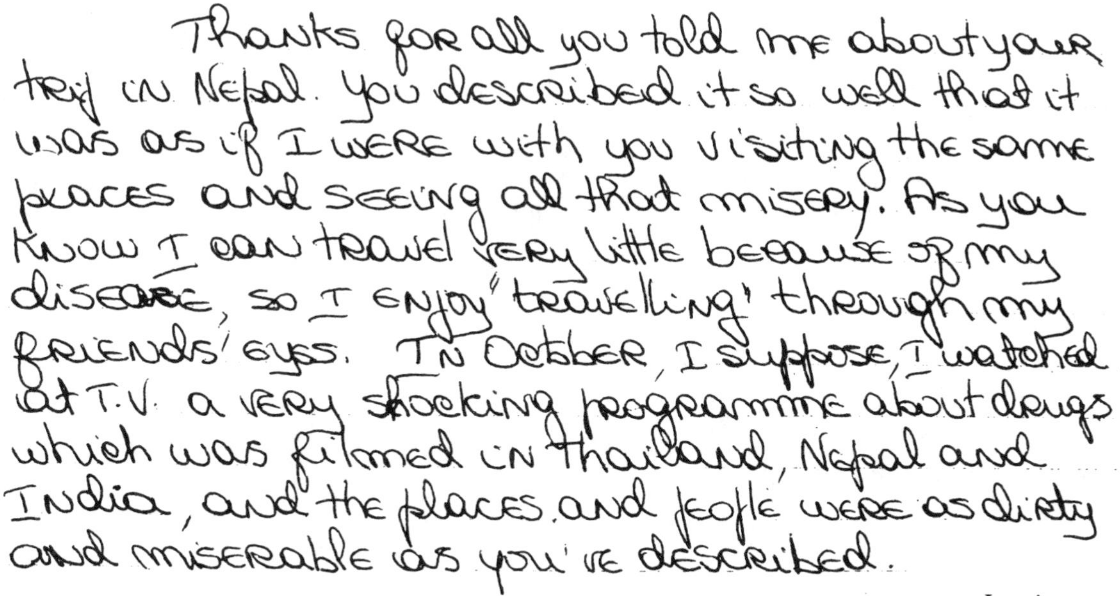

Thanks for all you told me about your trip in Nepal. You described it so well that it was as if I were with you visiting the same places and seeing all that misery. As you know I can travel very little because of my disease, so I enjoy 'travelling' through my friends' eyes. In October, I suppose, I watched at T.V. a very shocking programme about drugs which was filmed in Thailand, Nepal and India, and the places and people were as dirty and miserable as you've described.

Juanita

Spaces between Words

	Narrow	Normal	Wide
SOCIAL	*devotion* *need for social contact* *indiscriminate sociability* *uncritical* *impatience* *lack of social barriers* *lack of tact* *dependence upon environment* *lack of independence* *lives in the present* *suffocation* *feeling of deprivation* *impulsiveness* *(extrovert)*	*balanced adjustment* *stable social approach* *emotionality* *extreme tact* *warmth* *naturalness*	*shyness* *loneliness* *reserve* *unwillingness to make the* *acquaintance of others* *incorrect self-evaluation* *burdened, not free* *(introvert)*

INTELLECTUAL	*active imagination*
	ability to improvise
	activism
	unclear thought
	talkativeness
	difficulty in switching from
	  one topic to another
		clear thought
		sense of order
		good organizational skills
		sense of proportion
		quick judgment
		logic
		analytic thought
		ability to analyze
		  individual components
		  of complex subjects
			musical
			abundance of ideas
			ability to switch
			  from topic to topic
			undisciplined thinker
			loss of relevant connection
			  to issues
			few associations

Spaces between Letters

The absence of proper spaces between letters and words can make your handwriting completely illegible. There are cases (they are rare, but they do exist) in which the spaces between letters and words are not consistent, and then we read words different from those that were written.

Once I came across a letter of a mentally ill person (professional ethics prevent me from using his sample in this book), and I read the following sentence: "Me e t meat broad waystation." I couldn't make much sense out of this, especially since the script was almost undecipherable. After long hard work, I realized that the writer meant to write "Meet me at broadway station." Cases like this are very rare. Most people are careful to leave fairly clear spaces between letters, or at least between words.

The normal space between letters is the size of half a round letter. A smaller space would be too narrow, and a larger space is too wide.

There are occasions when you will encounter changes in spacing. This may be a temporary phenomenon, appearing in handwriting mainly when the writer is at a crossroads in life, and has not as yet decided about his future path in life. This characteristic vanishes when the writer makes a choice, ending this period of indecision. This is an additional reason why you should always try to examine more than one sample of a person's handwriting, written during various periods in the writer's life.

The interlinear spaces in Gunther's handwriting are large and exaggerated. Weak concentration is one of the character traits listed in our chart for large interlinear spaces. In Gunther's case, you can see that the spaces between the letters also become progressively bigger: the spacing in the first line is smaller than in the last line of the note. This shows a weakening of Gunther's concentration when he has to concentrate for a longer period of time. Other features of his handwriting, in addition to the fluctuating spacing between letters, reveal a lack of discipline, excitability, instability, and a weak will.

Greta has very narrow spacing in her handwriting. After checking other features in her writing, you will be able to state that she is tense, anxious, stubborn, suffers from a feeling of deprivation and "suffocation," and is egocentric and selfish.

Linda's handwriting also has narrow spaces between letters. This handwriting, however, reveals a sense of responsibility, concentration, sensitivity to criticism, and a lack of initiative – she doesn't even dare change the shape of her letters.

I WAS DELIGHTED TO MEET YOU BOTH IN BERLIN I THOUGHT YOU MIGHT LIKE THIS PICTURE

Gunther

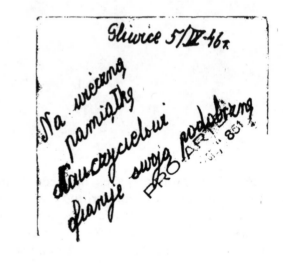

Greta

Thank you for the viewcard and the
I am enclosing our latest issue o
week, they depict the "year of the d
you certainly had a marvellous Ro
so many lovely memories to store f

Linda

Space between Letters within Word

Wide

alertness
optimism
imagination
initiative
devotion
frankness
thirst for achievement
creativity
enthusiasm
ability to improvise
weak concentration
mentally unfocused
hot temper
illusions
hysteria

Normal (medium)

alertness
developed self-criticism
concentration
stability
realism
clarity
creative tension
cautious implementation

Narrow

sense of responsibility
concentration
anticipation
tension
sensitivity to criticism
lack of daring
inner struggle
pettiness
anxiety
stubbornness
deprivation
feeling of suffocation
egocentricity
selfishness

Alternating, changing

weak will power
lack of concentration
difficulties in decision-making
impressionability
at a crossroads in life
high excitability
pretentiousness
weak discipline
lightheartedness
instability
lack of flexibility in areas of interest
disturbed concentration
disturbances in normal functioning

Alignment

We use ruled paper from the time we begin to learn to write until we leave school. The use of such paper should accustom us to write in straight, horizontal lines, even on unruled paper. But very few of us write in absolutely straight lines. If you come across a sheet of unlined paper with horizontal lines of writing, separated from each other by a constant space, your first reaction is to assume that the writer used a ruler. (The original meaning of the German word *Faullenzer*, which today is used for the ruled page, meant to be placed under the [unlined] page you write on, is a "lazy person"). The connection is quite clear. People who use a lined underpage think it is important to be seen as orderly. It is difficult to write in absolutely straight lines, so they make life easier for themselves by using a ruler. You cannot determine from this alone that the straight-line writer is lazy; you must verify this with other graphological signs.

There are two ways you can check this. One possible way is to put a ruler on the left side of the page, next to the margin. If there is a fixed interlinear space of 9-10 mm., you can be sure that the writer used a ruler. The second possibility is to fold the page in two. Now look at it from behind a strong source of light. Try to make two lines overlap. If all the other lines overlap as well, you can be certain that a ruler has been used.

Alignment had already been studied by the early graphologists. They saw the motion of your hand from the beginning of the page to its end as symbolizing your transition from the past to the future. Since the upper zone was considered to be the "good" one, ascending lines signified optimism, and descending lines marked pessimism. You can become aware of the writer's feelings by retracing the writing with a pencil or a closed pen. When you follow the movement of the writer's hand with your own, you feel optimism/pessimism, as well as other feelings, such as hesitation or energy.

The formation of lines undergoes changes in the course of a day, sometimes even while you are writing a single text. Your moods have an immediate effect upon your handwriting in general, and on alignment in particular.

It is difficult to find anyone who can write a straight line without the use of a ruler. Experiments which have been conducted have shown that blind people and people who do not look at the paper while writing are incapable of writing in straight lines. This would seem to indicate that straight alignment requires concentration and optimal control, as well as a great deal of optical attention to the page and the line on which you are writing.

Now we are going to learn how to examine alignment. Fold the handwriting sample in two, and place the bottom of the page on the first line, so that the two bottom, folded-over corners of the page will be parallel to the top corners. Now slowly start moving the folded part downwards. Make sure that only a part of the line is revealed. If you can see the right part of the line first, while the left part remains concealed under the sheet, this is a case of ascending alignment. If the left part of the line is revealed first, this is a case of descending alignment. If you can see a word here and there, this is a case of wavy alignment. The line may be concave, in which case the right and left ends of the line will be revealed, with the center still covered. If the line is convex, you will see the center, while the ends are still concealed.

When you come across ascending step-like alignment, it looks as if the writer were drawn upwards. If he had no self-control, the line would have continued to go up, but the writer did check himself, and returned to the original line. This symbolizes a return to reality. The same is true for descending step-like alignment. The writer resisted the force pulling him downwards, and his writing goes back in place at the beginning of the next word. You may find various combinations here,

Don't expect that the entire sample will consist of step-like alignment. If there are step-like alignments in a number of words in a row, then you must look for their meaning in the appropriate column of your table.
such as concave lines with descending alignment, or ascending alignment with a wavy line. In order to analyze such handwriting, you must take a number of character traits from a number of columns in your table; the more dominant graphological sign will represent a greater number of traits.

All of this applies to samples which were written on unruled paper. The following rules apply to samples written on a ruled paper:

If you find that the writing is "attached" to the ruled line, and all the letters "rest" on the line, this means that the writer is disciplined, does not dare break out of an established routine, and is not independent. You can rely on him only in petty matters.

When the letters are written above the line, you can assume that the writer has difficulty in following the beaten path, and that he seeks to be independent. There are several possibilities when the letters are written under the line: either the writer was tired, or he has a sense of realism, or possesses an especially developed sexuality. Your selection of traits depends on the other characteristics of the handwriting's sample.

The words in the line may look like:

ascending alignment

concave alignment

descending alignment

convex alignment

ascending step-like alignment

descending step-like alignment

Now let's look at some examples of different
kinds of alignment.

Straight alignment

a very bright and talented college student.
She is 20 yrs. old, right handed. She was vice
president of the student body this past year
By request, she painted a mural for the

Ascending alignment

I think it will be all for today, I
would like to write more but I am very
busy actually.
Anyway, I do hope this
letter finds you well, and that soon too

Descending alignment

My name is Diana Lynn Hubbard. I come from Blair WI, I'm recently living in New York. I've been here for ten months. And I find that I like it a lot. It's a lot different from Wisconsin. There's always something to do out here. Back there you have a hard time finding something to do.

144

Concave alignment

When we came back from our vacation,

Convex alignment

Today is Tuesday, January 29, 1980. It is the 87th day of captivity for the 50 Americans in Teheran, Iran. God knows when they will released alive from the American Embassy. In fact, the vast majority of the world is very angry at the occasion.

Wavy alignment

I hope you are have fun with your mother and father in Canada. Maybe I will call you when you come back.

Letters attached to the line

age rates will go up now from March 1.

I have not changed dolls with any of my new pals lately. In fact
I have not not got any dolls for a long time now. You say you
have send dolls to pals and never got the promissed one in return.

Letters above the line

LONDON HILTON
ON
PARK LANE

Date and Time: ... 6, 86   9.32

To: ... MRS KOREN

Room Number: 606

Letters below the line

This is the way I always write

145

An additional sign you may encounter, which you must interpret separately, is a line which falls at the end. In other words, the line starts out straight, but the last word drops. You can easily identify this sign, even without the folded-paper test. The writer may be childish, aggressive, or talkative. He gets caught up in the momentum of writing, and finds it difficult to go on to the next line. He squeezes in the words, until he absolutely runs out of room, and is forced to go on to the next line. Frank's letter is a good example of this type of alignment.

Now let's look at a sample I'm sure you can't read: it was written in Amharic, the official language of Ethiopia. Although you cannot conduct a complete graphological analysis without knowing the standard forms of the letters, you can still get a sense of the general atmosphere of the handwriting – and find some hints about the writer's personality – from the elements you can identify: interlinear spacing, margins, size, and pressure. You can see that the alignment is clearly convex.

Frank

Amharic writing

148

Let's look at this note written by the late Egyptian President Anwar Sadat in Jerusalem. You immediately see how sharply the lines rise. This tells you that the note was written when Sadat was in a burst of enthusiasm, when he was in a euphoric, optimistic mood.

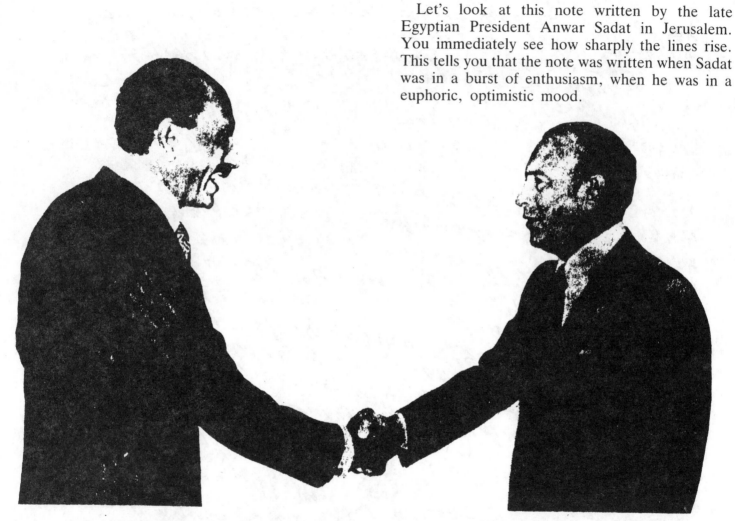

President Anwar Sadat is welcomed at the King David Hotel, Jerusalem by Mr. Yekutiel X. Federmann of the Dan Hotels Corporation.

KING DAVID HOTEL JERUSALEM

Thanks for the very warm
hospitality that we received
here.
My deep Gratitude
(to all the Staff.

لقد استمتعت أغمة بالأيام التي قضيناها

كل الشكر للنخبة الجميلة

الأمل
ميبا

٩٧٧/١١/٤

Anwar Sadat

Alignment

Straight
self-control
emotional stability
balanced actions
discipline
sense of order
self-criticism
perseverance
logic
attachment to one's goal
sense of duty
systematic
concentration
responsibility
suspicion
egocentricity
lack of openness
coolness
lack of feeling

Ascending
elation
enthusiasm
good feeling
happiness
ambition
ardor, drive
optimism
creativity
diligence
excitement
lack of peace of mind
frivolity
weak discipline
impulsiveness
aggression
authoritarianism
hysteria

Descending
speedy adaptation
desire for fulfillment
purposefulness
drive to achieve
tiredness
depression
disillusionment
pessimism
guilt feelings
melancholy
physical illness
feeling of inferiority

Falling at end of line
talkativeness
aggression
infantilism

Descending step-like
struggle against lack of courage
struggle against depression
weakened self-confidence
increased self-control
request for support
loss of faith
fear of failure

Ascending step-like
controlled impulse
fearful ambition
need of release
bad temper

Concave
gradual recovery
continually increasing effort
slow development of potential
empathy (emotional identification)
gradually increasing enthusiasm
struggle against depression
suspicious of oneself
bothersome
pest

Wavy
chaos
lack of stability
complex imagination
flexible adjustment
sensitivity
moodiness
indecision
hesitation
spineless
purposeless
lack of self-confidence

Convex
waning enthusiasm
tiredness
inconsistent alertness
persistent
enthusiasm without perseverance
ambition without perseverance
disappointment
fear of failure
insecurity

Writing below the line
sense of realism
weakening of concentration
developed sexuality

Writing exactly on the line
lack of independence
discipline
reliable only in petty matters

Irregular
jumpy thought
dramatic ability
originality
concentration problems

Use of ruler
desire to appear organized
lack of self-confidence
laziness

Writing above the line
desire for independence
stubbornness
avoidance of the beaten path
recoil from contact
no sense of reality

152

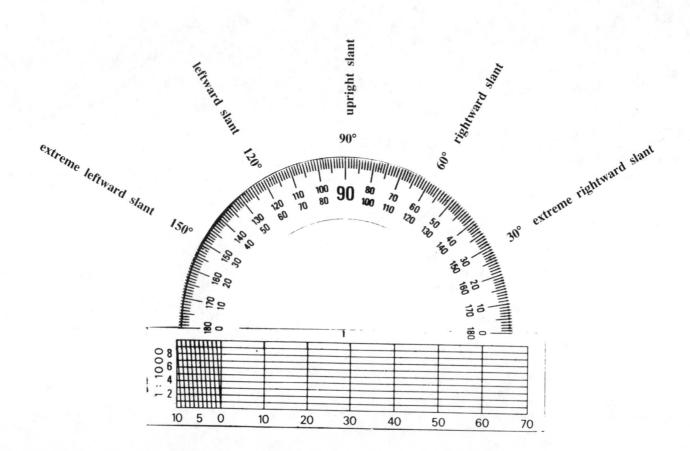

Slant

The slant of your handwriting reveals your attitude towards other people and society. If you are friendly, natural, and outgoing, your handwriting is very likely to be slanted towards the right.

You can measure slant with the aid of a protractor. Place the protractor on a line. If the paper is not ruled, align the protractor with the imaginary horizontal line produced by the handwriting. We measure the slant from right to left.

Rightward slant

The rightward slant is the most common, regardless of the language of the handwriting. This is true for English and the other languages written in Latin characters, from left to right, and for Semitic languages such as Hebrew or Arabic, written from right to left.

A certain slant can be predominant for an entire nation. Most Americans and Dutch write with a rightward slant. And indeed, they are known as friendly people, pleasant, quick to make contact with other people, who prefer action to philosophizing and deep thought.

The rightward slant is more suitable for extroverts, whose energy and interest are directed outwards, towards society. Their handwriting flows in the direction of other people, in the direction of the ending margin (see chapter on margins), which stands for other people, the outside, and the future. Rightward slanters include people who come into daily contact with the public: doctors, nurses, psychologists, social workers, and so on. Many journalists, who are active participants in our society, and find themselves in daily contact with many people, also usually write with a rightward slant.

It is easiest for you to write with a rightward slant, because this slant coincides with the direction of your writing. It enables your hand muscles to move freely and quickly. Rightward slant writing is from the writer's "I" outward, to "you." This type of slant appears more natural, and less restrained, than any other slant you will encounter in handwriting.

Upright slant

The letters written with this slant are perpendicular to the line, i.e., at a 90 degree angle with the ruled line, or the imaginary written line. You can think of the letters as soldiers on guard duty. In fact, you will never encounter an upright slant of exactly 90 degrees. There will always be a slight rightward or leftward tendency. The upright slant arrrests the movement of your hand, and requires that you maintain extreme control of the entire writing process. Writing with this type of slant indicates cleanliness, aggressiveness, order, purposefulness, a practical sense, internal discipline, and a developed sense of responsibility. If we permit ourselves to make generalizations, these qualities are those generally attributed to the German people.

Fluctuating slant

More than 2500 years ago, the Chinese philosopher Confucius warned against people "whose writing is like a reed in the wind." Fluctuating slant indicates changing moods and difficulties in persevering. It is only logical that the more stable a person, the greater pains he will take to insure the uniformity of his writing. When the slant fluctuates, the writer gives free reign to the script, and does not use sufficient control. The greater the fluctuation, the less internal discipline possessed by the writer, and he has more difficulty in persevering and attaining his goals.

Leftward slant

It is difficult to write with a leftward slant. It goes against the hand's natural movement, and you will soon feel the strain if you try to make your hand muscles move contrary to their natural inclination.

Most adolescents try to adopt the leftward slant, but you will find that only a small percentage of writers (those whose personality actually corresponds to this slant) continue to use it after adolescence.

It was interesting for me to discover the connection between sex and slant. During the course of my research, I arbitrarily selected 5,000 handwriting samples, divided equally between men and women. I found that there were seven women writers with left-slanted writing for every male writer with this slant. On the other hand, I discovered that most of the samples of upright slant had been written by men.

If you look at your tables, you will find that left-slanted writing reveals caution, modesty, inhibition, self-control, a fear of the future, and retrospective "living in the past." The upright slant, on the other hand, usually signifies people who are objective and logical, with balanced opinions, and who are well-organized.

These characteristics match the usual stereotypes of men and women. Many psychologists trace the origins of these differences between the sexes to the socialization process. In other words, these differences in personality are due to the acquisition of different values and norms by men and women, starting from infancy, and their learning to fulfill different roles in society. We can conclude that if the trend towards equality between men and women continues, then the sex-related differences in handwriting will lessen or disappear. Much research still remains to be conducted on this issue.

As with all other graphological signs, you cannot consider slant apart from the other elements of someone's handwriting. Leftward slant, especially, cannot be analyzed as an isolated quality. The leftward slant is the most complex one, and is characteristic of the writers who are least accessible, both to graphologists and psychologists.

In many cases, left-slanted writers tend to be introverted, isolated from society, and wrapped up in themselves.

A special type of writing you may encounter begins with a rightward slant, but "straightens out" towards the end:

Lefthanded Writers
How should you treat the slant in handwriting by people who are lefthanded?

As a general rule, you should optically "amend" the slant back to the right by about 10 degrees. In other words, you will treat a handwriting sample which has an upright slant as if it had a rightward slant of 80 degrees, and a sample with a slant of 100 degrees is to be treated as if it had been written with a slant of 90 degrees. Starting from a slant of 100 degrees, treat the handwriting as being left-slanted.

This type of slant is characteristic of rash people who charge ahead, oblivious to obstacles. Their highly developed senses stop them on the brink of danger, when they straighten out and stop. These are the people who "almost drowned," "almost ran over a child," "almost fell," and so on.

Another handwriting type you may run across starts with a rightward slant, straightens out in the middle, and finally takes on a leftward slant:

This type of writing is caused by the writer not lifting his elbow while writing. It is characteristic of lazy or tired people, who do not want to, or have difficulty in, lifting their elbows, which are fixed during the whole process of writing.

Now let's look at two pairs of handwriting samples, written by people who are completely bilingual, in both speech and writing, in Hebrew and in a language written in Roman characters (either English or Rumanian). Look at the slant; you will see that it is the same in both languages.

Marc writes with a strong rightward slant, about 45°, in both Hebrew and Rumanian. Of course you should measure both samples in the same manner, as we have learned.

Jerry writes with a fluctuating slant, in both English and Hebrew.

Marc

Jerry

When I first became interested in graphology, I was surprised to discover that slant does not change with language, even though Hebrew, for example, is written from right to left, the opposite direction to English.

I raised this question during one of the first handwriting courses I taught, since I still could not explain this puzzling phenomenon. One of my students suggested the following explanation, which seems to me to be more satisfactory than any other:

In the transition between languages, the handwriting is turned around twice; if you turn something around twice, you will return it to its original direction. For example, the only English letter which has a "twin" in the Hebrew alphabet is the letter "N," corresponding to the letter *Mem* in Hebrew. The letter "N" begins in the left bottom corner, and *Mem* starts from the top right corner. We have turned the letter around twice, with it returning to the original slant.

Now lets look at a few more examples of different types of slant.

Evelina writes with a leftward slant, and her handwriting exhibits an increasingly leftward tendency. Her slant is also unstable – it becomes upright on occasions, before returning to its leftward direction.

This is to tell you how happy we'll be to travel through the hills and the valleys of our

Evelina

Paul's handwriting has a rightward slant.

*Peter is here also facing
The weather here has been
hot and very humid. Hope
to see you all very soon.
Best regards to all the family*

Paul

Richard writes with a strong rightward slant.

We arrived in New York at eleven this morning. The weather is nice, but, the drivers are your type, very reckless. Bet you would enjoy the mess. Hope you and Jane are having fun. Be careful and we will see you Thursday —

Richard

Kamil writes with an upright slant, of exactly 90°.

Sales and administration in an import firm specialising in spare parts for vehicles. In this firm I had great experience with

Kamil

Slant

Rightward	Leftward	Upright	Fluctuating slant
quick grasp	*caution*	*objectivity*	*moodiness*
emotionality	*modesty*	*emotions controlled by logic*	*insecurity*
ambition	*inhibitions*	*balanced judgment*	*worry*
sincerity	*lack of daring*	*good organizing ability*	*lighthearted, impressionable*
naturalness	*self-control*	*thoroughness*	*lack of independence*
friendliness	*attachment to the past*	*practicality*	*restlessness*
emotional involvement	*fear of the future*	*precision and order*	*instability*
empathy	*conservatism*	*moderation*	*conflicting decisions*
devotion	*guilt feelings*	*restraint*	*lack of perseverance*
submission	*self-torment*	*self-control*	*adventurousness*
warmth	*defensiveness*	*self-discipline*	*capricious stubbornness*
flexibility	*pretense*	*responsibility*	*childishness*
quick adjustment	*unnaturalness*	*perseverance*	
enthusiasm	*suspicion*	*self-criticism*	
dynamism	*foppery*	*will power*	
sociability	*intrigue*	*power of resistance*	
ability for self-expression	*compulsiveness*	*stubbornness*	
activism	*self-righteousness*	*concentration*	
gullibility	*faulty sense of reality*	*thorough thought process*	
recklessness	*selfishness*	*suspicion*	
eagerness	*arrogance*	*passivity*	
talkativeness	*mental tension*	*pride*	
stormy temperament	*haughtiness or feeling*	*strictness*	
superficiality	* of inferiority*	*egocentricity*	
impulsiveness	*hysteria*	*lack of interest in environment*	
lack of logic	*(introvert)*	*collector*	
lack of inhibitions		*lack of emotional involvement, coldness*	
weak self-discipline		*(introverted)*	
instability			
aggressiveness			
hysteria			
(extrovert)			

Handwriting Size

You have to distinguish between small, medium, and large handwriting, based on the height of the written letters. Small letters are less than 3 mm. (about 1/8 of an inch) high, medium letters are about 3 mm. high, and tall letters are higher than 3 mm. The letters you measure are the unizonal letters, such as e, i, n, and s. You must always measure these letters when they appear in the middle of a word (we will treat the letters which appear at the beginning or end of a word separately, in a special chart).

Handwriting size changes with age. Children's script is usually large, since their coordination is not yet fully developed. If you see that a child's handwriting is small, you should try and discover the reason for this size.

During adolescence there is a tendency to experiment with one's handwriting. You will discover that quiet, introverted teenagers usually acquire a miniscule script. This tendency is usually temporary, and changes after a short period of time.

Adult handwriting size can tell you about the writer's self-esteem. It is logical that large handwriting indicates a greater sense of the writer's own worth, while small handwriting indicates to us a more modest self-appraisal, and possible feelings of inferiority.

Handwriting size also tends to correspond to the writer's attitude to his environment. Someone with large handwriting usually sees everything as "big," "fast," "close," and "impressive." Small handwriting, on the other hand, indicates to you that the writer sees everything on a smaller scale, in a detailed, critical, and matter-of-fact manner.

Normal, average size handwriting indicates a balance between the writer's demands of himself and reality. He is usually well-adjusted, without ambitions that exceed his true abilities. This type of writer is satisfied with his lot.

On occasion large handwriting characterizes people who enjoy being in the limelight: actors, artists, politicians, teachers, and lawyers.

Elizabeth Taylor's handwriting is larger than average, and her signature is even bigger than her handwriting. There is a great deal of momentum in her script, indicating to us the need to be seen and a tendency to exaggerate. You can see that she is stormy, energetic, she ignores petty details and has a very strong desire to be noticed. These traits certainly correspond to the biography of this movie star.

Elizabeth Taylor

Jack's handwriting is especially large. You can conclude from this that he needs wide open spaces, and that he finds it difficult to operate in crowded places. He is an active person, gets excited easily (every experience grows within him), and it is important for him to prove his capabilities.

Now is the time for all good men to come to the aid of the party. The quick brown fox jumped over the lazy dog's

Jack

Smaller handwriting is more characteristic of scientists, philosophers, researchers, and people with strong religious feelings. It seems that these people feel "small" in relation to the world and Creation. You will discover that small handwriting is also typical of disciplined and obedient people, who adjust well to set frameworks. I have examined many samples of soldiers during basic training. Their handwritings were usually small; the size of the letters were of one or two mm. less than their usual size during this period.

You immediately see that Sheila's small handwriting appears cautious. Sheila acts in a systematic, thorough, and analytic manner. You can conclude that she takes small details seriously, and that she is comfortable in small places.

& folks. We're all fine here, thanks. I'm afraid whether you can still remember me. Yeah! You see, it's so long since I last sent you my news! But you see, I've had serious problems recently that enabled me to send as to you as to my other pals any new. I'll explain all that mess further on, ok?

First of all I want to thank you for your most welcome and long letter, for the two cards, for the luggage tag and for the letter that came in just a little after my birthday, but as it is said " Before late than never ", I want to thank you

Sheila

Handwriting size

Large (higher than 3 mm.)	**Small** (less than 3 mm.)
self-importance	*modesty*
desire to be conspicuous	*humility*
pride	*restraint*
conceit	*obedience*
need for independence	*control*
festiveness	*thoroughness*
activism	*matter-of-factness*
enthusiasm	*family feelings*
persuasiveness	*sense of duty*
broad-mindedness	*realism*
generosity	*research oriented*
devotion	*keen observation*
lacking realistic sense	*precision*
rich imagination	*balanced judgment*
exaggeration	*preference for minute details*
uncritical attitude	*pedantry*
superficiality	*pettiness*
illusions	*lack of initiative*
frivolity	*feelings of inferiority*
lack of concentration	*cowardice*
eagerness to please	*dry personality*
lack of caution	*narrow-mindedness*
stormy temperament	*religious tendency*
wastefulness	
impulsiveness	
jealousy	
ill tempered	
hysteria	
megalomania	

Changes in Size within a Word

Now we are going to learn how handwriting size may vary within the same word.

The beginning of a letter stands for the writer's self, and reflects the writer's feelings concerning his own worth.

shrunken beginnings

will bring for both you & l success. We are embarking on a new line that l hope

exaggerated beginnings

Dear Erma,
Please Read And
THEN   CALL   ME

irregular beginnings

Dear Hans —

Funny how we met, never-
theless, 'all has turned out for
the best.

Munich is so far away
but I have faith that distance
is no barricade.

exaggerated endings

As stated in our previous discussions, we
have run the course. When we meet again
I hope our interactions will be meaningful.
Last time we met we had a hard

diminishing endings

Belatedly, I want to thank you for so kindly typing the
analysis of my handwriting at the time of your program
appearance with Alan Douglas at WKYC.
I have been intrigued with this art for about ten years —

regular size

the next valley, no concept of the world outside and live in fear of "payback" death and sorcery. They still have tribal wars fought with bows and arrows. The government has tried to suppress these but it is a very difficult task as the areas are so remote and the mountainous terrain is very hard to cross.

Some of these transcripts make shocking reading for all who consider the Presidential office as embodying the highest ~~best~~ ideals of our land. Others of these conversations must be

Tina

Tina's letters do not vary in size. Each letter of the alphabet resembles the other examples of the same letter in shape and size. Check one letter after the next, and compare them with each other: you will find that in addition to our general impression of similarity between the written characters, elements of different letters are identical, such as the shape and size of the circle in the letter "U" and the letter "O." You can see from this sample that Tina has a stable personality. She is disciplined and persevering, conservative, tries to avoid doubts, and is afraid of change.

irregular size

We are on earth. to Love + lerne.
let not the ~~pleasure~~ pain that comes
  with pleasure
out balance comedy of life

   There are sharp fluctuations in the size of the
letters in John's handwriting; you can see that there
is no uniformity here at all. Both size and pressure
vary, and there are slant changes. These and other
characteristics in John's writing indicate a great
deal of tension, restlessness, anxiety, difficulties in
decision making, adventurousness, and rebellion.

I would like to enjoin
we intend going love of Tuscany on the
10 of January ~~for~~ weeks in order of
celebrate the 80th Birthday of my
Mother.

John

Recibí del Sr. Amito Cancino J. la suma de CUARENTA pesos ($ 40—) moneda nal, valor de 1 espejo consignador para la venta con la Sra. Estella de Cardozo.
Bogotá, 29 de enero de 1943.
María Eugenia Cardozo.

Mario

I met "Mario" in Bogota, Colombia. I went into an antiques store, as I do in every city I travel to, and asked to see postcards or old manuscripts. The saleswoman showed me some postcards, which I bought. In the meantime I wandered around the store. I came across a portfolio full of old receipts, documents, and manuscripts. I asked the saleswoman (who knew about 10 words of English) if I could buy the portfolio. She laughed and told me that these were documents which had belonged to her father, who had died thirty years ago and that she couldn't possibly sell them. When she saw the disappointment written all over my face, she told me – in sign language and by facial expressions – to choose one document. When I chose Mario, she gave it to me as a present. I would like to thank that saleswoman by dedicating this chapter to her.

You can see that the initial letters in Mario's handwriting are noticeably bigger than the other letters in his handwriting. According to our table, he is haughty, conceited, and very self centered.

Equal/stable
stability
inner discipline
self-criticism
power of resistance
perseverance
consistency
self-control
responsibility
cautious planning
precision
well-developed memory
avoidance of doubtful situations
conservativism and conventionality
lack of originality
innocence
fear of change
stubbornness
lack of vision

Irregular
tension
anxiety
restlessness
inner struggles
hesitation – difficulties
 in decision making
suspicion
undermined discipline
insecurity
feeling of inferiority
adventurousness
unopinionated
rebelliousness
hysteria

Exaggerated beginnings
need to appear in public
self-awareness
need to be supported
high self-esteem
talkativeness
arrogance
conceit
feeling of superiority
need to feel self-important
demanding
ambition

Shrunken beginnings
simple manner
humility
modesty
warmth
gradual realization
 of personal potential
undemanding
respectfuul
low self-esteem
insecurity

Exaggerated endings
openness
persuasiveness
ability to interpret
kind-heartedness
daring
courage
ambition
inconsideration
need to have the last word
egocentricity
vulgarity
demanding
aggressiveness
blame of others

Diminishing endings
tact
politeness
courtesy
quick grasp
shyness
flexibility
caution
adaptability
quick orientation
quick adjustment
self-restraint
avoidance of commitment
suspicion

Width – Narrowness

You do not have to be an expert graphologist to distinguish between John and Martin's handwritings. In John's handwriting the letters are very wide while in Martin's they are very narrow. The samples you will analyze will not always be as clear, and the differences will not always be so striking. You will have to measure the samples, and calculate the ratio between the horizontal and vertical length of the letter. The slant of the letter is of importance, and you must measure the letters in accordance with their slant.

John

Martin

If the width of the letters equals their height, we say the width is normal. If the width of the letters exceeds their height, the letters are wide. If the width of the letters is smaller than their height, the letters are narow.

The width of the script emphasizes the horizontal line. The movement of a wide script is towards the outside, other people, and the ending margins. It symbolizes activity.

Narrow writing emphasizes mainly the vertical lines. It suggests restraint, inhibitions, and, sometimes, bitterness and aggression.

Diana reduces the height of her letters, almost to the point of turning them into a horizontal line. Her handwriting is flat, and, even without measuring them, you can see that the letters are very wide.

Diana

By way of contrast, look at these two examples of narrow writing.

Width – Narrowness

Wide script

ambition
consistency of purpose

sharpness
broad perspective
sociability
sincerity
freshness
broad-mindedness
seeker of independence
good organizing ability
spoiled
demanding
extravagance
materialism
arrogance
superficiality
impatience
rashness
imprecision
weak self-control
love of comfort

Narrow script

restraint
moderation
shyness
modesty
balanced judgment
self-control
creative tension
ability to concentrate
ability to improve
limited activity
feeling of "suffocation"
fearfulness
compulsiveness
inferiority complex
selfishness
suspicion
lack of interest in the surroundings

Alternately wide and narrow script

insecurity concerning goals
contradictory decisions
perplexion
inflexibility in areas of interest
unstable self-confidence

Connection – Separation

Your handwriting may be completely unconnected, separated, and legible, or it may be so
connected as to be completely illegible. The connectedness of the letters is of secondary importance, compared to the letters themselves. If the
connectedness becomes the primary element of a
person's handwriting, the handwriting becomes
illegible.

Unconnected script, which resembles the way
you were taught to write in school, is easier to read.
People who write this way are usually clear
thinkers. They are also liable to be conventional
and unoriginal; their ways of thinking probably
won't stray far from conventional paths. They also
tend to be critical, and they have analytical minds.

People whose writing is connected are a different
story. They are faster, and more alert to what goes
on around them. The degree of connectedness
shows you the degree of the writer's adjustability to
society, and his ability to connect things. If you
encounter exaggerated connectedness, however,
this may indicate that the writer is afraid to let go of
his pen, thus expressing insecurity.

A person's handwriting may contain "air
bridges," which you will need a magnifying glass to
identify. These bridges are produced by the writer's
lifting his pen at the end of a letter, and putting it
on the paper again at the beginning of the next
letter. In other words, the writer creates a "bridge"
in the air with the same movement that would have
produced a written connection if he had not lifted
the pen from the paper. Sometimes you can see the
hint of a line at the end of a letter, leading in the
direction of the next letter, with the same line (its
continuation) picking up at the beginning of the
next letter.

Some graphologists, such as M. Ivanovic and
Max Pulver, claim that air bridges should be
regarded in the same manner as connected writing,
and I agree with this opinion.

We all have learned a great

it quite frankly amazes us all.

of us here tonight understand

of respect and admiration

Michael

Thanks for the

hospitality Kat

here

My dear

Anwar Sadat

Michael's handwriting seems to be almost completely unconnected. He possesses a sharp intuition, together with a tendency towards research and in-depth analysis. While he is blessed with an intuitive grasp of things, he is also willing to work hard, to conduct research to verify his intuitive conclusions. He is very precise, sensitive, objective, responsible, independent, has lots of ideas, and is sharp and critical.

You can find an abundance of original, swift connections in the handwriting of the late Egyptian President Anwar Sadat, despite the fact that English was not his mother tongue. It seems from this sample that he could write English so well that he could create original connections.

If you look at your chart, you will find the following qualities for Sadat: a talent for dealing with people, quick adjustability, sociability, a sharp mind, quick associative ability, the ability to organize and coordinate, practical sense, a systematic approach, alertness, a realistic understanding of the connections between things, conceptual thinking, and occasional aggressiveness.

This is almost a complete report, based on only one graphological feature! But I must remind you that this is not the way to prepare a proper graphological report. You must check the other elements of the handwriting sample before reaching your final conclusions. (We will continue our analysis of Sadat's handwriting in the following chapter.)

Connectedness

Connected	Unconnected
talented approach to people	*intuition*
quick adjustment	*independence*
friendliness	*abundance of ideas*
intellectual sharpness	*shrewdness*
quick associative ability	*discarding of things as they are*
good organizing ability	*sense of humor*
ability to coordinate	*research orientation*
acceptance of things as they are	*visual memory for details*
practical sense	*precision*
superficiality	*balanced ambition*
alertness	*objectivity*
ability to perceive logical connections	*responsibility*
realism	*inner struggle*
conceptual thought	*anxiety*
lack of inhibitions	*absentmindedness*
impulsiveness	*unfocused thought*
feeling of deprivation	*tension*
aggressiveness	*adjustment problems*
high excitability	*critical attitude*
insecurity	*sensitivity*

Writing Forms

There are four basic shapes of writing and forms connecting the written characters: the garland, the arcade, the angle, and the thread. You will find that these basic forms may also appear in various combinations. In such cases, you must try to determine the dominant form, that is, the most frequent form, then the second most frequent form, and so on. The connective forms also may vary a great deal.

In this chapter we will learn about these connective forms and signs.

You should be able to find one of these forms in your own handwriting. This is the form you decided to adopt after outgrowing the pattern you were taught in school. It will appear throughout your writing, both in the letters and in the connections between the letters.

garland   *arcade*   *angle*   *thread*

The Garland

The garland has two main characteristics: its middle zone leans downwards, on the bottom of the line, and it is open at the top, looking like an open cup or a bowl. It is a soft form, one which is easy to write. The garland indicates a good-natured disposition, kindness, sincerity, and the desire to communicate. It is written in a spontaneous, natural manner, and it accordingly suggests spontaneity and naturalness.

An angular garland may occur in two shapes: 1) an external garland (facing out) with an internal angle (facing in). The garland is directed towards other people, and expresses warmth, softness, and love. The inside angle, on the other hand, is directed towards oneself, and reveals inner rigidity, stubbornness, and adjustment problems. The angular garland may indicate a lack of sincerity, or the fact that the writer has made a conscious effort to acquire qualities which are not part of his intrinsic nature.

2) an external angle with an internal garland. The angle is directed towards other people, and indicates a sincere writer, who exhibits stubbornness and coolness. The inward-facing garland points to a different internal composition. It indicates a sensitive person, with a much more delicate character than you would assume on the basis of a casual acquaintance with him.

Words may also be connected by garlands. This is one of the most sophisticated connective forms. In certain cases, you will find that it renders the script less legible.

You can identify many garlands in Timothy's handwriting. His writing is quick and spontaneous. Despite the fact that there is some fluctuation in the angle of writing (which detracts from his general stability), his writing shows that he is a kind-hearted person, willing to acknowledge the existence of other people. He adapts quickly, and empathizes with those around him. From your table you will see that emotionalism also suits him (he is very stormy, quick, and emotional).

personal message you are looking for in this section — are you looking at my handwriting or are you looking at the content of this message. I certainly do appreciate the opportunity to go through this analysis since I have not done it before.

Timothy

You will also find many garlands in Morris's handwriting. He places much emphasis on the social realm (look at the spaces between rows, words, and letters. Sociability just pours out of every graphological sign here.) Morris is a true social animal. He is a party-goer, and is full of humor and warmth. Look at the especially nice garlands in the letter "E" in the word "Enclosed" and the crossbars in the "t"s.

Notes from a Jewish Grandfather

West Palm Beach
Jan. 10/83

Dear Sam, Alice

Enclosed you will find some zerox material in reference to my hobby of Party going over the period of years. I sent it to your place so you can have something to read while you are waiting for all the workers to come in to buy Som Furniture. Stay well and take it easy. I am feeling O.K after that nightmare I had on Christmas Eve (over)

(Moisha Pippick)

Morris

You will find deep, supported garlands in Danielle's handwriting. She is childish and dependent. Her emotional inhibitions are clearly visible. You must also, however, take into account Danielle's age (a freshman in college). Her handwriting will undoubtedly change as she grows older.

at college – Mt. St. Marys college in Emmitsburg, Maryland. I am at New York city on a Mid Term Break, with my parents. I am very interested in this process of analyzing a persons handwriting.

Danielle

In President Ronald Reagan's handwriting you can see an interesting combination of angular garlands and another graphological sign, fluctuating angles. You will find that the characteristic of being impressionable appears in the tables for garlands and for fluctuating angles. The more thoroughly you examine additional graphological signs, you will discover additional facets of the President's character. The fullness and roundness of the script, together with a developed middle zone and the garlands, point to goodheartedness, willingness to acknowledge the existence of others, emotionalism, and childishness.

I was raised in the Christian Church which as you know believes in baptism when

Ronald Reagan

But now you are in for a surprise. The angle table includes leadership ability, ability to withstand pressures, self-discipline, aggressiveness, decisiveness, and similar traits. The angle with strong pressure table also includes leadership qualities, determination, decisiveness, vigor, particularly strong stubbornness, and aggresiveness. If you look closely at Reagan's handwriting, you will see that the script is not hard enough to justify the traits of particularly strong stubbornness and other signs of aggressiveness.

You will undoubtedly ask, and rightly so, how can two such contradictory types of traits – impressionable and decisive – appear in the same handwriting, with both of them appearing as dominant traits? President Reagan's handwriting provides us with a classic example of the rule that you must never conduct a superficial graphological analysis. You must compile a list of all the graphological signs appearing in the handwriting. When your list is complete, you must make use of the knowledge you will have acquired in psychology and the experience you will have gained. All this will help you to build a firm base for your intuitive insights. Now you can produce a thorough, balanced analysis. Reagan's tendency to be impressionable does exist, but it is limited to certain circumstances, and stays within certain bounds. Beyond these limits he becomes more firm and aggressive, and can withstand pressures.

Now look at Reagan's signature. The initial "R" is considerably bigger than the other letters, even if we take into account that it is a capital letter. This shows us his need to appear in public and be popular.

Going on to yet another level of analysis, you will note the threads which appear in Reagan's handwriting. In the table for threads, you will find many qualities, including speedy comprehension, happiness, alertness, political sense, diplomatic talent, and acting talent.

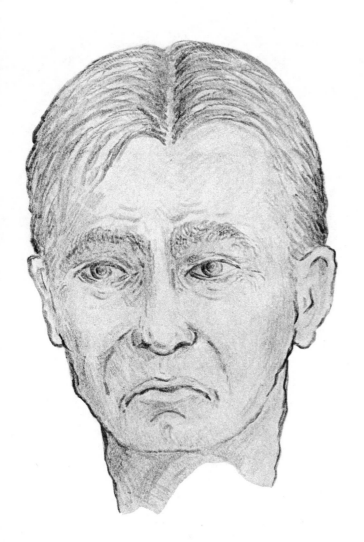

The Arcade

The arcade reminds you of a roof, a cover, or a hand protecting a head (see the chapter on symbolism). The main purpose of the arcade is to provide cover, in order to protect the writer from external factors.

The person who writes with arcades will not adjust spontaneously to new social contexts. He may not be genuine; he may conceal his real feelings. If you encounter arcades in a child's handwriting, you must try to find out what is happening to the child. If a child uses arcades you can be almost certain that he is repressing something deep inside. This is not all: this tendency may worsen with age.

The arcade is constructed in such a manner as to close off all zones except the lower one, which is the distress zone. This is the center of all repressed feelings, reflecting disturbances in our daily functioning, of which we are unaware, in most cases.

You can see clear arcades in Lorraine's handwriting. She even manages to turn a garland into an arcade: look at the bottom part of the letter "L" in the word "last." An arcade appears where you would normally expect to find a garland. This teaches us of the presence of strong defensiveness. Many of the traits in your arcade list will reappear as traits of the other graphological signs in her writing. Her letter creates an atmosphere of restraint, defensiveness, and slowness.

new apartment. Even tho it isn't very big, you should be able to have a good time. We are having a fun time in New York. Last night we took a horse drawn carraige ride around Central Park.

Lorraine

Another interesting feature of Lorraine's writing is the fact that she turns most of her garlands into straight lines. Her pen turns a normally round letter like "u" into a square.

Joan's handwriting has lower-zone arcades. This indicates the presence of concealment, especially in sexual matters. At the same time, you will also find hard angles in her handwriting, most of which are also in the lower zone. You can learn from this that her behavior patterns are well-formed and very stubborn, which suits this zone.

and I found it most interesting. I especially enjoyed the ending where you said you had gone to Spain and seen the bull fights. Your reaction to them was

Joan

The Angle

Angles are rigid. hard, and inflexible. Graphological reseach has shown that it takes three times longer to produce an angle than a garland. Angles slow down the writing process, since they force the writer to interrupt the flow of his movement in order to change direction.

This connective form may indicate hardness and stubbornness, as well as leadership potential and stability. Writers who use angles are not afraid of challenges, and they do not shy away from having to make an effort. You can rely on the angle-writer to fulfill his tasks efficiently.

The direct connection is another connective form which bears some resemblance to the angle. You will also find this connection in the handwriting of people who take a calculated approach to others, in order to serve their own personal comfort and selfish interests. Direct lines or connections are also very characteristic of aggressive people, especially if the lines have thick ends, like a spreading oak tree.

Al

Al's handwriting is composed of harsh, uncompromising angles. Now take another look at Bismarck's handwriting (page *40*). You will see that most of the script, and the manner in which it is connected, is composed of especially harsh angles.

As a general rule, it is difficult to form relationships with such unyielding people.

The handwriting of another famous person, Sigmund Freud, is also composed mainly of harsh angles. You will find angles in the handwriting of many leaders and other people who successfully separate their private and public lives. These are people who do not recoil when confronted with opposition. They do not blindly follow the crowd. These are the people who succeed in changing the world, and in having many other people follow them.

Sigmund Freud

You can find another type of angle, not leadership-oriented, in Fred's handwriting. The angles in his handwriting, like his handwriting in general, are not consistent. His angles look very much like spasms. Fred is a very stubborn person, with firmly formulated opinions. On the other hand, he has no pretensions of changing the world. He does his work, and he doesn't care what other people say and think about him. He'll continue doing things his own way and at his own pace.

DEAR HANNA,
    HERE IS A SAMPLE OF MY HANDWRITING,
WHICH I AM GIVING YOU TO LOOK AT AS
YOU LIKE AND TO THINK ABOUT IN
YOUR MANNER,

Fred

You will find softer angles (although not totally lacking in stubborness) in the handwriting of Felix Klein. Felix is a 75-year-old graphologist who works, acts, responds, and feels like a young man. He is active, still works at least twelve hours a day, and always feels excellent. Those around him are always caught up in his enthusiasm, vigor, originality, and humor. His writing is quick, spontaneous, and full of vitality. The angles in his writing are a result of his vitality, purposeful approach, creative thought, and ability to withstand pressure.

17.) Is the occupation of special importance to society?

18.) At what age are workers considered "through"

19.) How may the occupation be rated as a way of life?

Felix Klein

Threads

The thread does not have a clearly defined form. Its shape changes, and it is not easy for you to identify this type of form. If you make an effort to write each letter separately, writing slowly and clearly, there will not be any threads in your handwriting. If, on the other hand, you write quickly and carelessly, you are very likely to find threads in your handwriting. Like any other graphological sign, you must look at the entire handwriting sample when you examine threads.

A graphological thread, like the one you use when sewing, has a special property. It can crawl into the tiniest opening, and is comfortable anywhere. It adjusts well to new situations. You can bend it, or change its direction, but it will always retain its original form.

You will find threads in the handwriting of politicians and people with diplomatic skills. They also appear in the handwriting of hysterical or "spineless" people.

Apologies for taking so long.

a "real" situation, I can turn

Marc

The handwriting of Marc contains beautiful threads, made by a light hand, exhibiting both agility and flexibility. Marc holds a Ph. D. in psychology and graphology. The threads in his handwriting obviously point to speedy comprehension, happiness, alertness, quickness, vision, and speedy adaptability.

I wish I could have had the opportunity to attend these conventions at an early stage...

Daniel

You can find many different kinds of threads in Daniel's handwriting. The threads in this sample point to Daniel's well-developed business sense: Daniel is a bank manager.

Thanks for the very warm hospitality that we received

Anwar Sadat

The handwriting of the late Egyptian President Anwar Sadat contains an interesting combination of threads, arcades, angles, and garlands. You can find something applicable to Sadat in each of your tables. Sadat had the ability to coordinate (he brought about the peace between Egypt and Israel), as well as being polite, well-mannered, discerning, sociable, empathetic, tolerant, and compromising – all traits drawn from garland connection forms. He possessed "arcade" traits such as restraint, self-control, politeness, caution, and self-criticism. From the table ascribed to the angle forms we can draw forcefulness, thoroughness, logic, responsibility, self-discipline, the ability to withstand pressures, and leadership ability. From the table ascribed to threads: speedy comprehension, quickness, adaptability, political sense, diplomatic ability, originality, intuition, understanding of others, flexibility, wit, business sense, acting ability, shrewdness, and realism. Look at the tables. You will see that most of these qualities were taken from the threads table. And indeed, threads do appear as the dominant feature in Sadat's handwriting.

Connective Forms

Regular garlands
kind-hearted
acceptance of others
adaptability
ability to coordinate
sincerity
naturalness
simplicity of manner
flexibility
sociability
empathy
sensitivity to the needs of others
politeness
devotion
tolerance
ability to compromise
ability to make concessions
discernment
optimism
impressionable
emotional
softness
dependence – lack of independence
lack of self-discipline
instability
laziness
weak-willed
lack of framework
light-heartedness
superficiality
childishness

Supported garlands
emotional inhibitions
tendency to depend on others
immaturity
need of support
dependence

Deep garlands
crisis
depression

Angular garlands
pretense
warmth, concealing hardness
(or the opposite – depending
on the location of the angle)

Arcades
restraint
self-control
balanced judgment
politeness
shyness
caution
self-criticism
defensiveness
inhibitions
sense of form
reserved
aesthetic sense
artistic talent
doubtfulness
haughtiness
external adaptability
feeling of discrimination
concealment
gossip
intrigue
artificiality
dishonesty
insincerity
pretense
coquettishness
selfishness

Angles

forcefulness
perseverance
decisiveness
thoroughness
order
logic
self-discipline
practical sense
purposefulness
stability
responsibility
planning ability
creative thought
morality
leadership ability
critical attitude
ability to withstand pressures
composure
rigidity
stubbornness
pedantry
compulsiveness
inflexibility
coolness
lack of consideration
aggressiveness

Angle with strong pressure

leadership ability
energy
determination
decisiveness
forcefulness
acute stubbornness
aggressiveness

Threads

speedy comprehension
happiness
alertness
agility
vision
adaptability
political sense
diplomatic talent
originality
intuition
spontaneity
understanding of others
flexibility
wit
business sense
acting talent
insincerity
shrewdness
shrewd tactics
evasiveness
intrigue
impulsiveness
realism
superficiality
tension
tendency towards hysteria

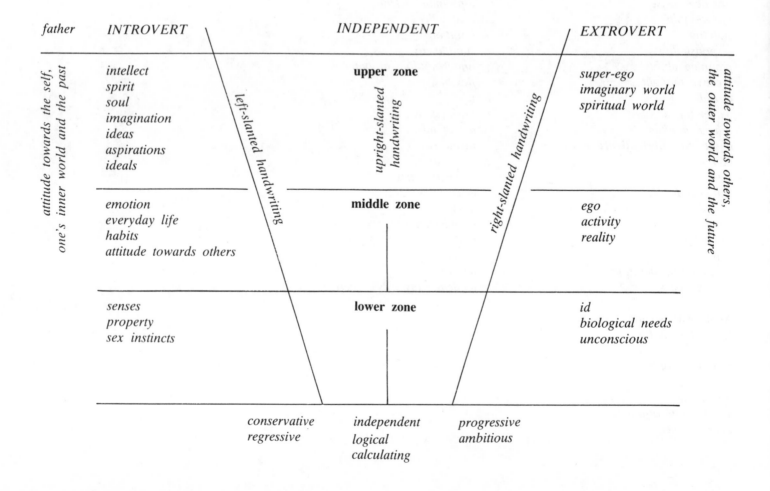

The Zones

typical upper zone letters: f, t, l, i-dots, t-bars
typical middle zone letters: a, n, o, w
typical lower zone letters: f, g, p, y

Max Pulver was the first graphologist to divide handwriting into zones. Most graphologists use this division, which has not undergone significant changes since Pulver devised it in 1930. I have added a few additional elements to Pulver's basic chart, in order to give you a more sophisticated, and possibly clearer, picture.

The chart is divided according to basic concepts which appear in our thinking, our understanding, logic, and our collective subconscious. Some of the concepts mentioned in our table appear in an ancient Kabbalistic work (Kabbalah is Jewish mysticism). The division between right and left, up and down had similar significance for the ancient Kabbalistic authors as for the modern graphologist.

From a very early age you hear, and absorb, the association of "up" with good; both God and Heaven are above us; progress is depicted as moving upwards. The upper region is thereby connected in our consciousness with ambition, the acquisition of knowledge, ideals, and deriving from it, with the father figure. In many cultures, the father was responsible for teaching his children. He was associated with education, aspirations, and principles. Although this association may appear primitive to us, and certainly flies in the face of modern conceptions concerning equality of the sexes, it is still deeply rooted within us, and you cannot ignore its effect upon people's handwriting.

The middle zone is connected with daily functioning, emotions, habits, and social interaction. Our relationships with people are very important, since there are very few people who seek constant isolation.

The qualities represented by the middle zone play an important role in our daily life. For example, when you meet a friend and ask how he or she is, you receive an answer which is directly connected to this zone. The answer may be "Fine," "Not well," or "Very well"; it usually refers to the person's general feeling or mood – his emotional state. You won't receive an answer like "I am smart" or "I am rich," since the answer comes from the emotional, rather than physical or intellectual, sphere. It should come as no surprise to you that the middle zone is the most prominent zone in handwriting. Most writing is concentrated in, or at least starts from, this area.

The lower handwriting zone contains everything popularly associated with the nether regions. The subject of sex, which had been taboo for many years; suppressed instincts; the underworld; hell; earth (property, survival) – we usually associate all these with the lower zone.

The middle zone is largely neglected in Fred's handwriting, while the other zones are developed, but not systematically.

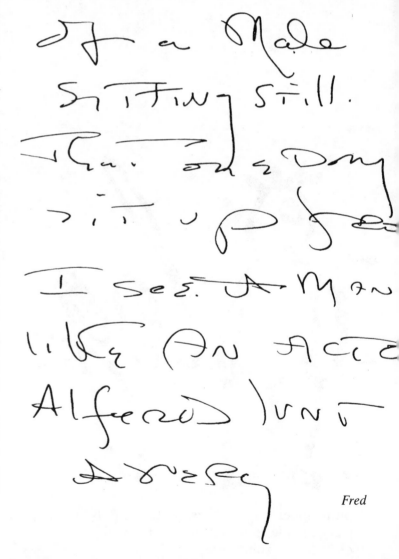

Fred

In Dina's handwriting, the middle zone is especially developed, while the upper and lower zones are undeveloped.

One day, before lunch, they went for a walk. While they were out, a little girl named Goldilocks found their house and went in. When she

Dina

The lower zone in Larry's handwriting is especially developed.

Larry

The lower zone in Harvey's handwriting is quite developed, while the upper zone is neglected. Look at the letters "t" and "f" (marked by arrows). Harvey exhibits few of the qualities listed in your chart under "prominent upper zone," but may possess many of the qualities listed under "prominent lower zone."

Harvey

All three zones of Barbara's handwriting are developed in an exaggerated manner, especially the lower one.

head of thoughts. I almost fell asleep - was very nice and relaxing. I guess I'll go

Barbara

The upper zone is developed more than the other zones in Ann's handwriting.

The interesting thing which i noticed about the stage band was the way in which the audience particip. along with the players. This seemed to

Ann

210

You can see in both Shelly's and Elizabeth's handwriting that the lower zone is especially developed. You can conclude from this that each of them has an exaggerated preference for the material-existential spheres of life; each of these women, however, will outwardly express this preference in a different manner.

Shelly goes down to the lower region, comes back up a bit, goes around and goes on. This distortion of the lower zone apparently reflects an individualistic and uncompromising stance on sexual matters. Her opinions and conduct are not influenced by society and those surrounding her.

In Elizabeth's handwriting, on the other hand, you see that the lower zone is swollen, but with weak pressure. This shows you that her conduct is not necessarily realistic, but tends more towards her fantasies (this is also corroborated by the bubbles in the upper zone of her handwriting).

Are you acquainted with the cartoons by Helen Hoskins that have appeared in the New Yorker magazine? Her subtle humor is delightful.

Shelly

I am curious to know what you think of my handwriting. Many have said that they can barely read my ... is good luck!

Elizabeth

Prominent upper zone	Prominent middle zone	Prominent lower zone
spirituality	*emotionally rich*	*aspiration towards fulfillment*
high intelligence	*kind-heartedness*	*research-oriented*
quick grasp	*kindness*	*thoroughness*
creative ambition	*sensitivity*	*profundity*
vigor	*enthusiasm*	*systematic approach*
enthusiasm	*love for people*	*seeking anchor*
adherence to principles	*willpower*	*practical planning*
curiosity	*aesthetic sense*	*realistic approach*
seeking independence	*realism*	*technical ability*
positive attitude	*joie de vivre*	*domination*
fanaticism	*concern for reputation*	*tiredness*
planning ability	*childishness*	*possessiveness*
critical attitude	*innocence*	*materialism*
striving towards the higher spheres	*inflexibility*	*hoarding*
sublimation	*jealousy*	*disappointment*
seeking spiritual compensation	*domination*	*stubbornness*
feeling of deprivation	*egocentricity*	*strong instincts*
need of prominence	*sensitivity to criticism*	*sexual drive*
escape from reality	*selfishness*	*adjustment difficulties*
feeling of inferiority	*laziness*	*pretentiousness*
adventurousness	*hysteria*	*(influence of mother)*
(influence of father)	*"there is no one like me"*	
	parasitism	

Height Differentials

In order to examine differentials in letter height you must know the standard letter size of the language in which your sample is written.

Significant height differentials indicate a great deal of ambition and a refusal to accept conventional forms.

You will find it interesting to examine people's handwriting at different points in their lives. People who used to be very ambitious, and who had significant height differentials in their youth, may change as they age, with the height disserentials in their handwriting gradually becoming smaller. (Although this is a frequent occurrence, do not take this as a general rule!)

Now let's look at some specific examples.

Brigitte writes with small height differentials. Most of the table is suitable for her: she is quiet, moderate, makes do with what is available, and knows her limitations.

spät und ich bin müde. Ich schlafe momentan sehr schlecht und am Morgen fällt es uns dann schwer, aus dem Bett zu

Brigitte

214

Despite Oscar's being 72 years old, his handwriting has large height differentials. He is very ambitious (try to imagine what he, and his writing, must have been like at the age of 20!). You will find that almost all the entries in the "Large height differentials" table suit him.

I love life, people, events and I fight for principles and right now I'd move troops in on SAUDI ARABIA

Oscar

Betty's height differentials are small, and she is interested in only a few subjects.

We have attended 2 shows and have been to numerous "tourist" sights.
Will see you when we get home.

Betty

Jim writes with large height differentials. You can use most of the table for him. He is very ambitious, takes the initiative, acts spontaneously, and is not quiet. He acts impulsively and needs prestige; this and other signs in his writing point to an hysterical disposition.

I enjoy having professional people analyze me. Often this helps bring events into perspective.

I am left handed and was born Christmas Eve 1937 (Capricorn). My field is finance, and I am CFO

Jim

216

Although Wanda's writing also reveals large height differentials, you can only use the top portion of the chart for her. She is more restrained than Jim, and the bottom portion of the chart is not appropriate for her. We can only use ambition, initiative, desire for change, and activism.

as I was very busy getting our new home ready. We were married on August 20 th It was a real beautiful day sunny & cool, a rarity for Aug. We traveled through the New England States heading destination, Prince

Wanda

Large
ambition
initiative
spontaneity
restlessness
lack of tranquility
desire for change
activism
problems of concentration
lack of proportion between
 desires and abilities
impulsiveness
dissatisfaction
compulsiveness
exaggerated demands
disregard of other people
desire for prestige
tendency to hysteria
(extrovert)

Small
inner calm
willingness to be satisfied with little
modesty
logic
down-to-earth
satisfaction
balance between desires and abilities
knowledge of own limitations
morality
mature opinion
moderation
perseverance
sense of responsibility
ability to concentrate
slow absorption
discipline
passivity
laziness
phlegmatic
apathy
(introvert)

Varied
(in relation to, different samples
of the same letter)
faulty inner consistency
alternating between
restlessness and passivity
insecure relationship between the "I"
 and the writer's role in life

Direction

It is not sufficient to measure the length and the continuity of the letters in a handwriting sample. You must also examine the direction of the letters. As I have already mentioned, the upper zone is connected with the father image. Since it is the region of the superego, it reflects discipline and morals. The lower zone, on the other hand, is linked to the senses – the survival instinct, continuity, procreation, and sex, which are connected with the mother image. (See the chapters on symbolism and zones for more details.)

When the direction of the script fluctuates, this may indicate to you a lack of inner tranquility, tension, difficulties in choosing a specific direction in life, insecurity, and difficulties in communicating with one's environment. If you see different directional trends within a particular zone, you should interpret this in accordance with the qualities of that zone.

Ruth

In Ruth's handwriting you can clearly see the forward direction of her script. There is no doubt that her writing is rapid. She saves time by not lifting the pen from the paper, even between words. Most of the qualities in our table suit her.

I really haven't got a clue what to write about especially as Lee is looking over my shoulder, but I suppose a few lines of rubbish will do. Enough rubbish is enough so I'll sign off with my

Maureen

Maureen's handwriting goes in strange directions. She goes back and forth, which distorts the motion of her script. Since her movements are exaggerated, look at the last sections of both of the tables. If we add this information to the lower zone, which is swollen in a strange manner, and other odd characteristics of her writing, you can conclude that Maureen has a very complex personality.

You can detect a forward direction in Kate's handwriting, but she creates this movement after having turned leftward in a determined manner. Here also, you must consider both directions. Since the dominant direction is leftward, you should take more traits from the "leftward" table.

I want to go to Italy. The first thing I remember is a trip by plane to Holland.

Kate

Backward – leftward
selfishness
communication problems
adjustment problems
insincerity
concealment
egocentricity
past-oriented
emotional problems
materialism
sentimentalism
inhibitions

in the upper zone:
positive relationship with father

in the lower zone:
negative relationship with mother
(introvert)

Forward – rightward
swiftness
ambition
quick adjustment
yearning for social contact
altruism
activism
future-oriented
good will
sincerity
openness
initiative
impressionable
dependence

in the upper zone:
negative relationship with father

in the lower zone:
positive relationship with mother
(extrovert)

Elaboration – Simplification

Elaborated handwriting is the product of adding lines, circles, and other elements which are not part of the basic form of the letters. These additions reveal a person's desire to decorate his writing and make it more beautiful. Elaborated handwriting reveals a well-developed imagination, a strong aesthetic sense, and the ability to graphically perceive objects.

Simplified handwriting, on the other hand, is produced by the deletion of certain unimportant elements of the script; in some instances, you will find that the letters are barely hinted at: long loops and lines are omitted, with the writing becoming narrow and thin. Simplified handwriting should suggest to you the writer searches for shortcuts, has a clear and practical way of thinking, wit, and a quick, "to the point" grasp of things. You may also find that simplified writing is typical of people who feel that they have revealed their potential to the whole world, and that they are successful in their undertakings.

Let's look at all the different possibilities for a letter.

simplified   *normal*   *elaborated*

[Marc's handwriting sample]

Marc

[Ronnie's handwriting sample]

Ronnie

You will find that performers and artists often have elaborated handwriting, and scientists frequently have simplified handwriting.

Marc's writing is a classic example of simplified handwriting. If you take traits from the "Threads" table, add the traits you will find in the "Simplified" table in this chapter, and the traits in the "Quick handwriting" table in the chapter on the writing speed (even an unprofessional eye can spot the speed of Marc's writing), you will be able to draw a detailed portrait of Marc's character.

Ronnie's handwriting is also extremely simplified. You can see that it is also fast and original. We can conclude that Ronnie is highly intelligent and is capable of abstract thought. He is capable of simplifying processes. He obviously thinks clearly and can make clear objective judgments, has a sense of proportion, has good taste, is original and quick. You will find all these qualities in the table for simplified writing, with verification from the table for speedy writing. You can easily imagine how thorough and detailed a character analysis you will be able to compose after using all your tables.

simplification

Hope you have come to stay for a while.

Fifth Generation is a company

Lucy

Now let's examine Lucy's handwriting, which is elaborated, with occasional ornaments and exaggerations. Look at the initial "W." It goes up in an exaggerated manner. The letter "H" (marked by an arrow) also is very elaborated. Lucy has dreamed all her life of being an actress. She obviously is very talented, but her need to follow the crowd is responsible for her remaining a secretary, for the present. You can easily see her ambitions in her handwriting. Take another look at the "H." With a little effort, you can see in your mind's eye an actress soaring through the sky.

Richard's handwriting is a celebration of loops, curlicues, and additions that actually lessens the legibility of the script. You can conclude that Richard has a well-developed imagination, possesses obvious artistic talents, is apparently unrealistic, and tends to exaggerate matters.

Nous passons un samedi excellent avec Mireille et une de vos très bonnes amies qui s'appelle Rose

Richard

elaboration

Betty's handwriting goes entirely to the other extreme. It is so simplified that it is what graphologists call "neglected handwriting," which is even worse than merely careless handwriting.

Betty

Simplification – Elaboration

Simplified handwriting

abstract thought
wisdom
simplification of processes
cleverness
lucidity
clear judgment
sense of proportion
objectivity
good taste
originality
practical sense
fastidiousness
utilitarianism
quickness
excessive concern
conservatism
tension

Elaborated handwriting

concrete thought
imagination
hedonism
cordiality
kind-heartedness
attentive to small details
greed
slowness
laziness

Ornamented handwriting

rhetorical talent
comparative imagination
optimism
artistic talent
literary talent
creative imagination
excessive strictness
desire to please
engagement in fantasies
materialism
lack of realism
exaggeration

Writing Speed

The concept of "writing speed" is not an absolute, quantitative concept. You must know people with speedy movements who produce poor results, and, on the other hand, people who seem to move in slow motion, but actually produce speedy, precise work.

I'll illustrate this with an everyday example. A worker enters his office and everybody knows he's there: he rushes in, throws his coat on the rack, almost jumps into his chair, throws everything around on his desk looking for a document to sign, slams drawers in and out looking for a pen. He talks a hundred words a minute, tries to hold three telephone coversations at the same time – and is so tired by 4 p. m. that he can't even lift a paper clip. Another worker takes his time walking into the office, neatly places his coat on the rack, takes his time getting his desk organized, has a cup of coffee, and takes one thing at a time. He has time for everything, doesn't rush – and by 5 o'clock his "Out" tray is twice as full as that of his noisy, "speedy" neighbor.

If you ask each of them to give you a writing sample, both of them are likely to write speedily. The first one, however, will make changes, and unnecessary movements, while our second worker will not.

"Quick writing" for the graphologist is an unrestrained movement which is rapidly flowing forwards without making any backwards or superfluous motions.

In contrast with what you have already learned concerning normal letter size and width, there are no standards for handwriting speed. There is a danger that the person examining handwriting speed may introduce subjective elements into his examination. We tend to judge speed on the basis of our own handwriting. If you have decided that your handwriting is "quick," then you will probably classify any handwriting slower than yours as "slow," even if it is actually quick by graphological standards. The "Determining Handwriting Speed" table will help you to make objective evaluations of speed.

A person's handwriting speed may vary. If you write under pressure, or try to write down every word of a lecture, you will write faster than when you want to produce a neat, legible script. This is the reason why you should never analyze the handwriting of someone writing under pressure, or a sample of material that had been dictated.

Writing speed reveals a person's inner rhythm. A person who works quickly, has swift emotional reactions, and walks quickly will probably write fluently and quickly.

Robert Saudek claimed that speed is the starting point of all graphological analysis, and devoted much effort to conduct an in-depth study of speed. In order to determine speed he produced extremely complex charts based on 26 rules. I have based the following tables on Saudek's tables. The tables in this book are extremely simple and clear, and you will find it very easy to use them as an aid in graphological analysis.

On rare ocasions you may encounter a handwriting sample containing an identical number of features from both the "Fast" and "Slow" tables. You can assume in such a case that the writer possesses the character traits of both a fast and a slow writer.

Determining Handwriting Speed

Feature	Quick	Slow
stroke structure	smooth, continuous line, without angles or trembling	broken, rigid, angular, shaky line
alignment	descending, ascending, or wavy	straight or ascending, wavy
left margin	widening	straight or gradually diminishing
width	wide script	narrow script
angle	rightward	straight or leftward
direction	forward-rightward	backwards-leftward
word endings	diminishing	exaggerated
forms	garlands, threads	arcades, angles
size	large	small
connectedness	3-4 letters connected	unconnected, each letter separate
pressure	even, average, or becoming stronger	weak or uneven
pressure nuances	needle-like	trunklike
oscillation	oscillates	well-organized
height differentials	average	small or, alternately, exaggerated
elaboration – simplification	simplified	elaborated, with additions and harpoons
punctuation marks	period resembling comma	precise, full, round, static periods
placement of i-dots and t-crossbars	inaccurate	precise

Now that you have learned to distinguish between slow and fast writing, let's look at some handwriting samples written at different speeds.

You will have no difficulty in determining that Rachel's handwriting is slow, even without referring to the table.

As Nira may have already told you, I have decided to withdraw from the internship program. Although we mutually decided that I should stay nearly two weeks ago, I have reconsidered that decision and arrived at the conclusion that it is in my best interest to withdraw. Despite my hopes, I do not think that it will work out. I stopped in to tell you yesterday, but you weren't in and now I am on my way to Tel Aviv for a few days. -- therefore, this note. I have already notified the CCIS office

Rachel

*rary approach via the supposed shoe crisis since history...
in principle of that amenity gauss by ambulatory intervention as it may... durationally, then characteristically. presumably, if, one misunderstood correctly., the brief model of inventory, eft mannerisms hereunder since the transactional problems incur as a economic deal toward humane conditions...*

Steven

Steven's handwriting is extremely slow, almost to the point of being compulsively so.

Anne writes very slowly, and takes pain with each and every letter. Her writing reveals order, precision, and careful planning of her every step.

You can state on the basis of this sample that all her actions are very slow and that she has difficulty in improvising, going from one subject to another, or in being original or agile.

studying physiotherapy, but that doesn't give me enough satisfaction so I really would like to do something completely different for one year.

Besides I think this is a very good opportunity to get to know another country with other people.

I like children and I have experience in how to keep them amused because I have worked as a volunteer in a sort of youth club.

Anne

Jeremy, on the other hand, writes quickly, and Debbie's handwriting is even quicker. Her sample reveals agility, the ability to improvise, and originality.

Jeremy

Debbie

Quick Handwriting

quick and abstract thought
ability to improvise
vision
activity
quickness
energy
alertness
spontaneity
self-confidence
sincerity
naturalness
devotion
generosity
openness
excitability, enthusiasm
optimism
ambition
emotionality
desire for change
restlessness
oversensitivity
hastiness
impulsiveness
lack of tranquility
impatience
superficiality
lack of planning
domination
extravagance
quick temper
easily tempted
contempt
tendency towards hysteria
lack of stability
(extrovert)

Slow Handwriting

concrete thought
concentration
matter-of-factness
logic
tranquility
mental stability
responsibility
peace of mind
sense of proportion
caution
perseverance
calmness
self-control
critical attitude
utilitarianism
slowness
endurance
passivity
hoarding
slow decision making
insecurity
repression
concealment
weak-willed
pretensions
rigidity
clumsiness
laziness
difficulty in understanding
narrow-mindedness
economy
pettiness
selfishness
egocentricity
greediness
fantasy
phlegmatism
apathy
anxiety
(introvert)

Writing Pressure

In the previous chapters we examined two dimensions, the horizontal and the vertical. Now we will add a third dimension – depth.

Writing pressure is similar to a handshake. A handshake, the contact of your hand with that of another person, may be either strong or weak. A person's handshake is not always indicative of his actual physical strength or appearance. You have probably met many pale, weak people with strong handshakes. The message conveyed by their handshakes is different from that conveyed by their physical appearance. The same is true of writing pressure. Your pen (or other writing instrument) makes contact with the surface of the paper, and the script is engraved by means of a certain amount of pressure. The degree of your writing pressure is not necessarily linked to your physical strength.

You can measure writing pressure in either of two ways. The first is the touch method. Turn the page over, and feel its reverse side. Some types of handwriting leave no impression on the back of the page, even on thin paper (you must take paper thickness into account). On the other hand, some people's handwriting leaves an impression, a type of Braille script, on the reverse side of the paper, and even on several of the next pages.

The second method requires the use of a magnifying glass, preferably with good light, so that you can distinguish between different degrees of pressure. If the writer used a fountain pen, you will see a "Mayer's socket" (named after its discoverer) under your magnifying glass. The socket will be between the two dark lines left by the nib of the fountain pen when it spreads under pressure. The ink has "spilled" between these two lines, leaving a strip which is lighter in color than the lines themselves. The more distant the lines appear to you, the stronger the writing pressure.

Most people do not use fountain pens today, so we will concentrate on samples written with ball-point pens (it is impossible to determine writing pressure in samples written with felt-tip pens and markers, therefore such samples should not be used for graphological analysis). When the writing pressure is weak, we say that the depth is "negative," i. e., the writing remains on the surface of the sheet. When there is strong pressure, the depth dimension penetrates into the paper (see drawing).

When the writing pressure is weak, the pen does not penetrate into the paper. Medium pressure will produce a slight penetration, without digging into the underlying sheets of paper or the writing surface. If you write with strong pressure, there is penetration into several layers of paper; sometimes the paper is even torn.

Different writing pressures are linked to different human spheres:

Weak pressure is connected with, and symbolizes, the spiritual/intellectual sphere.

Medium pressure is connected with the soul and emotion.

Strong pressure is connected with the libido, which maintains existence, and symbolizes the will to survive.

Enlarged cross section of paper (viewed from the side)

weak pressure, negative depth

medium pressure

strong pressure, high degree of depth

We also distinguish between horizontal (left-right) and vertical (up-down) pressure:

vertical pressure: *horizontal pressure:*

Make a few downward vertical lines, rest your hand for a minute, and then make a few upward vertical lines. As you have probably felt for yourself, it is easier for your hand muscles to produce a downward vertical movement, so these strokes will be stronger than the upward vertical strokes. Upward pressure in these strokes may indicate an illness or a mental disturbance.

Strong horizontal pressure points to a need to achieve goals quickly, a desire to take shortcuts, and the need for contact with other people. Strong vertical pressure reveals the need for in-depth thought, being firmly established, and a research-oriented mind.

The thick lines would seem to indicate strong pressure. A more thorough examination of the actual sample, however, would show you that there was no penetration into the paper, and a lot of ink was spilled on the surface of the paper. This is known as "pastosity", (simulated) pressure. You can produce this type of stroke by using a thick tipped pen, or by resting the pen on the paper at a sharp angle; thus a thick pasty line is produced.

Mathilda

Mathilda's handwriting pressure varies; it is at times strong, at times weak. Her writing pressure changes unpredictably. There is also a great deal of fluctuation in the slant of her handwriting. You can deduce from these two characteristics that her handwriting indicates a general lack of stability.

and feeling that it's about time that I make a change and try out a hot-weather climate. By coming to Israel I certainly got it! And now I don't miss the snow or the ice or the slush at all. In fact I'd rather sweat it out without clothes. There was at a time in my life, when I was younger when I used to spend hours just looking at

David

David writes with extremely strong pressure. He does not relax while writing ascending lines, and the entire script looks very tense, as if he couldn't loosen up his firm grasp of the pen. The pressure is so strong that it penetrated 8 sheets of paper (!) on the writing pad, and the writing was still legible on at least 5 sheets.

Strong pressure, especially when it is flexible and rhythmic, usually indicates self-confidence. In David's case, however, where the pressure is strong but not continuous, the writer seems to be afraid to relax his hand on the pen. This should indicate insecurity to you.

You can see that Maria played with varying degrees of pressure. She uses a particularly thick pen, and she turns writing into an art form. She presses hard on the pen. You can conclude that she possesses a great deal of vitality, ambition, and courage, she is intensely active, and enjoys being creative.

during "Siegfried
from Bayreuth
I wrote this analysis
of this Dr. Robert Wolf.
I cannot stand even
if he is tall and so
handsome.
You will be interested —
what we both thought
of his handwriting —
if you would come to
the same conclusion.

Maria

Danielle writes with very weak pressure. She is a very delicate woman, sensitive, with excellent intuition, but with no endurance. She is impressionable, and has difficulty in expressing a strong, decisive opinion and in advancing in accordance with her abilities. She is dragged along by external events, and does not act on her resolves.

There are many things in this world to appreciate such as the sun, nature and all the things that have been created to make our lives easier. We can choose a career from a variety of possibilities. We are given a chance to

Danielle

Phama also writes with weak pressure. Her character matches her handwriting: she is a delicate, sensitive, and empathetic woman.

So sorry you didn't get to visit us as planned. Maybe next time.
Hope you & your family have a joyous Christmas.

Phama

Strong

vitality
enthusiastic activity
ambition
courage
activism
inner vigor
emotional depth
self-control
readiness for action
joy of creating
decisiveness
self-confidence
excitability
physical strength
developed sexuality
stubbornness
impulsiveness
  (in quick writing)
heavy-handedness
talkativeness
  (only in slow writing)
aggressiveness
depression
materialism
selfishness
egocentricity
domination
inconsiderateness
tendency to undermine others
destructiveness

Medium

balanced activity
decisiveness
perseverance
stability
balanced judgment
quick perception
matter-of-factness
systematic
"down to earth"
will power
responsibility
politeness
self-confidence
self-control

Weak

delicacy
alertness
coordination
sensitivity
flexibility
quick orientation
tact
modesty
courtesy
politeness
empathy
tolerance
intuition
impressionability
unmaterialistic
instability
weak will
sexual weakness
weak resistance
lack of energy
indecisiveness
indifference
superficiality

Alternating

easily stimulated
lack of perseverance
firmness
impulsiveness
unsystematic use of energy
instability

Pastose

artistic tendency
ability to implement ideas
emotionality
cordiality
warmth
ability to find shortcuts
emotional depth
enjoyment of pleasures
sense of humor
well-developed senses
superficiality
laziness
self-indulgence
narcissism
feebleness

Discovering Illness through Graphology

After the Israeli-Arab Yom Kippur War in 1973 I was asked by a high school student to be her advisor for a research paper on graphology. I suggested that she write on a specific topic, rather than try and study the entire field of graphology in one year. We decided to examine the handwriting of Israeli soldiers before and after they were injured, in order to find out whether their injuries were reflected in their handwriting.

We went to hospitals and recovery centers for soldiers. In one hospital, I offered to look at a soldier's handwriting and tell him something about his character. Word spread quickly, and many soldiers, in different stages of recovery, asked me to analyze their handwriting.

One of the soldiers was completely covered by a blanket, and we could not see his injury. He was soon to be released from the hospital, and his wife asked me to analyze his writing. The bottom portion of the Hebrew letter *kuf* appeared to be cut off in his handwriting.

I asked his wife whether she happened to have a sample of her husband's handwriting previous to the time of his injury. His wife showed me a postcard he had written a few days before being injured. I was amazed. The same letter had a needle-like ending, with no hint of being cut off. Intuitively, I thought there might be some connection between the letter and his wound.

I asked the soldier, "Did they amputate your right leg?" "How did you know?" was his answer.

The upper zone of a person's handwriting corresponds to his head, the middle zone to the stomach, and the lower zone to the legs. A letter with a truncated lower zone may indicate an amputated leg, as was the case with this soldier – but why the right leg? Looking for the connection between specific letters and parts of the human body, I realized that the final *nun* looked to me like the left leg, and a change in this letter might indicate an injury to the left leg.

250

I began to examine handwriting samples, looking for the connection between handwriting and the writer's physical condition. I used a 10-power magnifying glass to search for spots, quivers, and other changes in handwriting. On the basis of my examination of handwriting samples and my many talks with different medical specialists, especially gynecologists, I concluded that information exists in the brain (and is reflected in our handwriting) before it reaches our conscious minds.

Pregnancy, for example, is expressed as a small spot in the pregnant woman's handwriting long before any external signs are visible. I examined handwriting samples written before, during, and after pregnancy, and I discovered that it is possible to detect the "pregnancy spot" between 48 and 72 hours after conception. This spot always appears very clearly in the woman's handwriting, in the middle (=womb) zone. It remains in her handwriting until the third or fourth month of her pregnancy, and then disappears. At this point, the middle-lower zone of the woman's handwriting becomes more rounded, full and feminine. The handwriting continues to swell up until the end of the pregnancy, with the letters then gradually resuming their original shape.

I met Rachel for the first time in New York. When I looked at her handwriting, I "diagnosed" her pregnancy. Her answer was, "I wish you were right." She had been trying to conceive for several months, and did not know that she had finally succeeded.

Once upon a time there was a beautiful young girl who lived with a wicked witch in a castle in the middle of the forest. She looked in her mirror every night, and asked her mirror "Mirror, mirror on the wall, who's the fairest of them all?" And one day the mirror said "Snow White".

Rachel I

Look at the first sample of her handwriting. We later determined that she had been pregnant for a week when she wrote this. You can easily see spots in the middle zone, in the letters "h," "w," and "n." Now compare this with the second sample, a letter she sent me after she had given birth: there is no trace of these spots in this sample.

Dear Chana,

Well, you were right! All's well here, The new baby is placid and quiet, and a good eater, which is all I could wish for at two weeks! I think of you often, and hope we can meet again on your next visit —

Rachel II

h   *sensitivity in head region*

f   *sensitivity in throat region*

e   *sensitivity in stomach region*

O   *sensitivity in left shoulder*

I   *sensitivity in spinal cord*

m   *sensitivity in kidney region*

night day

sentitivity or disability in right leg when spot appears at beginning or in middle of word; in left leg when it appears at end of word

It is not easy to accept any phenomenon that doesn't have a logical, "scientific," explanation. People who are interested in graphology ask me how a person's handwriting can point to his physical condition. They usually say that they can understand the link between handwriting and personality, but have a hard time accepting the possibility of a link between handwriting and diseases – even in the incubation stage.

It is hard to believe that handwriting can serve as an X-ray of a person's psychological and physical state. This is just one of the many questions I have been asking since I was four years old, without getting a rational answer. Who turns the earth? How can such perfect babies emerge from their mothers' wombs? Why does the sun go down at night?

There are many questions like this, and they all have the same answer: that's the way it is. These are hard facts, even if we can't explain why they happen.

You can find a "spot" anywhere on a letter. It is essential to distinguish between ink spots caused by a leaky pen, which are usually thick and smeary, and the spots caused by the writer's brain, which are small and often visible only under a magnifying glass.

When a truncated letter appears at the beginning of a word, this apparently is linked to an amputated right leg; when it appears at the end of a word, it is related to an amputated left leg.

Several graphologists have conducted in-depth studies on the connection between mental and physical health to handwriting. Alfred Kanfer's research on the detection of cancer, which he conducted over the course of many years in New York, has received wide recognition throughout the world. Kanfer showed that handwriting changes in various ways as a result of minor or serious illnesses. He demonstrated that high fever and a fast pulse increase writing speed, while a slow pulse rate and low body temperature reduce writing speed.

Crepieux-Jamin has shown that heart disease produces a small "fracture" in the upper loop of the patient's handwriting.

You can find a detailed account of graphology and diseases, especially on Kanfer's cancer research, in Huntington-Hartford's book *You Are What You Write*.

254

Martha's handwriting is an obvious example of handwriting influenced by a physical condition. You can see from this sample that the writer has difficulty in writing, and that her hand trembles a great deal while writing. Martha suffers from Parkinson's disease, and is almost ninety years old.

Martha

The paleness you see in Vivian's writing indicates general physical weakness. She was 81 years old when she wrote this sample. Although other signs which usually appear in the handwriting of people of this age – shaky handwriting caused by a trembling hand or sharp angles caused by inflexible joints – are not present here, her physical weakness is reflected in the weakness of her writing pressure.

You can see changes in the pressure of Tom's writing as it becomes weaker. Tom suffers from fluctuating blood pressure, especially from low blood pressure.

This is a very fine old building, and the Monday Afternoon Club is fortunate to have it as it's home. The rooms are very gracious, with high ceilings and beautiful wood-work. The

Vivian

Book Astrology, last chapter; it mentions that the Association publishes a monthly journal. I was wondering even though it says for members only,

Tom

I met Steve at Brooklyn College a few months ago. He made a great impression on me – he was intelligent, full of humor, friendly, open, and warm. When we spoke before he wrote this sample for me, he told me that he had seven Master's and Ph. D. degrees. He was 36 years old and divorced. I was fascinated by his learning capacity and asked him for a handwriting sample for the book I was writing. He quickly dashed off a sample. A quick glance showed me that there was a sharp gap between his signature and the rest of the text. The different size and momentum revealed that he was trying to present himself in a different light than what he really was. This was in total contradiction to the openness and candor which Steve revealed to me, and I was a bit surprised. I began to be worried when I took a second, more in-depth look at the sample. Even without a magnifying glass I could see sharp variances in pressure. Whole letters were absorbed and vanished, while entire portions of the sample were composed entirely of dots. Without going any further, I decided to ask Steve if he were on drugs. He admitted this on the spot, telling me that he was a heavy user of cocaine. I told him that his physical condition was deteriorating, and that he should see a doctor. He laughed at my advice, and said that he wanted a short but good life. A month after I wrote this paragraph, Steve didn't wake up. His death was apparently caused by heavy use of drugs.

My name is Steve Rappoport
I am one person in a million
I was in Vietnam for 1½ years
and I will never forget the

Steve

Another sad story connected with drugs was that of Joe and Dianna. Joe was a soldier who fell in love with Dianna while serving with the UNIFIL force in Lebanon. Dianna was the adopted only daughter of a psychiatrist. The mother was very concerned about Dianna, since Joe was her first boyfriend, and something she sensed set off an alarm.

Dianna and her mother came to me with Joe's letter. My first question was about drug usage. The mother said she would ask Joe and report back to me. In the meantime I began to analyze his handwriting, and I became convinced that Joe was indeed on drugs. The mother called me a few days later. She told me that she had asked Joe whether drugs were accessible to the UN troops. Joe laughed and said that although he was a medic, and had free access to drugs, the strongest drug he was ever on was the nicotine in his cigarettes.

Joe and Dianna split up a short time after I gave her my analysis. (Incidentally, I never provide direct advice. The work that I do, which I explain to my clients, is similar to that of a radiologist or a laboratory technician. The client has to make his own decisions; I merely provide him with the objective information he needs to make these decisions.) About a year later, Dianna's mother called me. She asked me to analyze the handwriting of her daughter's new boyfriend and asked, incidentally, whether I had heard that Joe had died. It turned out that Joe was a drug addict. When the secret came out, his UN unit sent him home, where he died a short time later from an overdose of heroin.

Joe

Testing Reliability

This is the most difficult work I face as a graphologist, not because of technical problems, but because testing reliability, more than any other personality feature, determines the fate of the person whose handwriting is being analyzed.

In some companies, for example, a prospective employee is not accepted if the employers are not totally convinced of his honesty. Businesses dealing with large sums of money will not hire any candidate if there is the slightest trace of suspicion concerning his trustworthiness.

You must therefore undertake this test with extreme caution, and use as many graphological elements as possible.

If you try and define "honesty," you will probably find it much easier to define the concept in negative terms: *not* stealing, *not* cheating, *not* conspiring, *not* trying to benefit unfairly at the expense of others. This difficulty may be due to the lack of objective standards for honesty. The definition of honesty varies from society to society, culture to culture, and even family to family.

Western society has seemingly rigid standards for honesty. It is generally agreed that it is forbidden to lie, to steal, etc. If it were not for these agreed-upon values, we would find it difficult to maintain relations with each other, or for society to function at all. But are these standards really so clearly

260

defined? If two or three people do something, you say that "everybody" is doing it. And how many times have you told a white lie in order to spare someone's feelings? Society accepts these attempts to generalize, to exaggerate, and to "modify" reality without any intention of harming other people. These deviations from an objective definition of absolute "honesty" are not regarded as "dishonesty."

The concept of absolute honesty does not exist in graphology either. Everyone's writing contains features generally indicating dishonesty; a person's writing may contain two or three such signs, but a complete analysis of his handwriting will show he is reliable.

Keeping this in mind, you must exercise the greatest caution when trying to find honesty or dishonesty, and determine the *number* of signs indicating dishonesty in the sample.

Obviously, the more indicators of dishonesty, the less honest is the subject; 7-8 signs of dishonesty indicate criminal tendencies. Isolated signs, even together with other isolated signs, do not indicate dishonesty.

This list of dishonesty indicators, is based on the works of Max Pulver, Robert Saudek, Rhoda Wieser, and other famous graphologists.

1. *slow writing (this does not include people who write slowly due to unfamiliarity with the language or illness).*
2. *general instability of the script*
3. *adherance to copybook style*
4. *upright script, tendency to fall to the left, or leftward slant*
5. *stressed initial letters*
6. *deleted letters or letter exchanges in slow writing*
7. *corrections which do not contribute to legibility*
8. *unnecessary points, with no meaning*
9. *covering strokes*
10. *broken letters, letters written with fragmented strokes*
11. *arcades*
12. *threads*
13. *harpoons, hooks*
14. *crossed lines*
15. *letters hanging in the air, ambiguous letters*
16. *complicated loops*
17. *letters open at their base*
18. *illegible signature, or one that does not match the handwriting*

1 Slow writing

2 General instability of the script

3 Childish handwriting

4 Upright, tendency to fall to the left.

5 Stressed initial letters   6 Deleted letters, excahanges

7 CORRECTIONS   8 unnecessary points.:

9 ~~covering~~   10 BROKEN   11 arcades

12 ~~in~~   13 hooks   14 o̊ å

15 letters harging   16 compleicoled loops   17 ∩ a

18

Testing Intelligence

I won't presume to enter the ongoing debate on the nature of "intelligence." For our purposes, we can rely on William Stern's definition that intelligence is the ability to capture the essence of a subject, to understand problems and find solutions on the basis of this understanding, and, thereby, to adjust to new situations.

As with any other trait, the more of the following features you find, the higher the intelligence level of the subject.

quick, spontaneous writing
rightward slant
easily connected (or connected with air bridges) writing
arcades
developed upper zone
weak pressure
small handwriting
simplified script
good division of space
proportionate fullness and leanness
normal spacing between letters, words, and lines
sharply defined script
no exaggeration of any kind
original handwriting
small signature

TONY COELHO, M.C.

E. THOMAS COLEMAN, M.C.

PAT WILLIAMS, M.C.

THOMAS A. DASCHLE, M.C.

LES ASPIN, M.C.

MICHAEL A. ANDREWS, M.C.

ROBERT S. WALKER, M.C.

VIC FAZIO, M.C.

JOHN R. MILLER, M.C.

RON PACKARD, M.C.

DAVE MCCURDY, M.C.

LEON E. PANETTA, M.C.

NORMAN D. SHUMWAY, M.C.

PETER J. VISCLOSKY, M.C.

GENE CHAPPIE, M.C.

STENY H. HOYER, M.C.

GLENN ANDERSON, M.C.

NORMAN Y. MINETA, M.C.

JIM OLIN, M.C.

DUNCAN HUNTER, M.C.

BARBARA VUCANOVICH, M.C.

DANIEL K. AKAKA, M.C.

JIM MOODY, M.C.

JOHN M. SPRATT, JR., M.C.

CARLOS J. MOORHEAD, M.C.

JACK FIELDS, M.C.

GEORGE W. DARDEN, M.C.

MATTHEW F. MCHUGH, M.C.

LANE EVANS, M.C.

RON RUDD, M.C.

DAN LUNGREN, M.C.

JIM COOPER, M.C.

JAMES V. HANSEN, M.C.

FRANK MCCLOSKEY, M.C.

DAVID S. MONSON, M.C.

DAVID DREIER, M.C.

GERRY SIKORSKI, M.C.

MARY ROSE OAKAR, M.C.

DAN GLICKMAN, M.C.

DON SUNDQUIST, M.C.

MARVIN LEATH, M.C.

AL SWIFT, M.C.

RICHARD H. STALLINGS, M.C.

BILL RICHARDSON, M.C.

E. CLAY SHAW, JR., M.C.

FLOYD SPENCE, M.C.

JIM CHAPMAN, M.C.

JAMES M. JEFFORDS, M.C.

ROBERT LINDSAY THOMAS, M.C.

THOMAS R. CARPER, M.C.

THOMAS N. KINDNESS, M.C.

JIM SLATTERY, M.C.

SHERWOOD L. BOEHLERT, M.C.

RICK BOUCHER, M.C.

J. ALEX MCMILLAN, M.C.

MICHAEL L. STRANG, M.C.

TIMOTHY J. PENNY, M.C.

BILL FRENZEL, M.C.

ED JONES, M.C.

JIM WRIGHT, M.C.

WILLIAM W. COBEY, JR., M.C.

ALBERT G. BUSTAMANTE, M.C.

JAMES H. QUILLEN, M.C.

E DE LA GARZA, M.C.

THOMAS S. FOLEY, M.C.

D. FRENCH SLAUGHTER, JR., M.C.

HAROLD L. VOLKMER, M.C.

BERYL ANTHONY, JR., M.C.

JAMES L. OBERSTAR, M.C.

ED ZSCHAU, M.C.

JERRY LEWIS, M.C.

CHARLES W. STENHOLM, M.C.

JAMES WEAVER, M.C.

HARRY REID, M.C.

WM. S. BROOMFIELD, M.C.

MARGE ROUKEMA, M.C.

DENNY SMITH, M.C.

TERRY L. BRUCE, M.C.

DENNIS E. ECKART, M.C.

TOM LANTOS, M.C.

ROBERT A. BADHAM, M.C.

WILLIAM E. DANNEMEYER, M.C.

HOWARD C. NIELSEN, M.C.

ROD CHANDLER, M.C.

The Signature

Your signature provides the graphologist with a better picture of your personality than any description of your character could ever do. But your signature does not exist in a vacuum. It doesn't mean much without your handwriting. You were taught all the letters of the alphabet in school, along with spacing and margins. Every first-grade classroom has a chart with the shapes of all the letters. You were probably taught to start such-and-such a distance from the edge of the paper, or you started out with ruled paper, with the margins already marked for you.

Your signature is an entirely different matter. No one taught you how to sign your name, nor did anyone choose a signature for you. You created your own signature, after many experiments and doodles.

Your signature undergoes many changes as time passes. Although your signature basically remains the same, you never sign your name twice in exactly the same manner, even during the same period of time. If a lawyer shows in court that two signatures are exactly identical, the court may decide that this is a sufficient proof that one of them is a forgery.

Your signature is accepted in today's world as your personal representation. Your signature on a check changes it from a piece of paper into money. A judge's signature can send someone to jail for life; a governor's signature may save a prisoner from the electric chair; a psychiatrist's signature may determine whether someone will live in society or be hospitalized. Contracts take effect only after they are signed. Billions of dollars may change hands on the strength of a few scribbled letters. Try to imagine a world without signatures: society as we know it would cease to exist. It is not surprising that graphologists have their hands full with real or suspected forgeries.

Above all, your signature symbolizes the real you – your inner self, your ego. A signature consists of one or more of three elements:

first name   last name   additions

It may change with age, marital status, and social standing. It may change many times, and in many ways, during the course of a lifetime.

Your last name represents your image in society, while your first name relates more to your individual ego. If you stress your first name in your signature, this may be an expression of a need to attract attention, or an urge to prove yourself. This may be a sign that the writer may not rely on his family, and wants to be judged on his own merits. If the first name is blown up, and is bigger than the writer's last name and/or the written text itself, this may indicate egocentricity and narcissism, or self-love. If the writer stresses his family name, this may symbolize family pride or dependence upon his immediate environment, i.e., the family.

At times you will come across a signature which is identical to the writer's handwriting, with the first name and last name written in such a way that they possess the same characteristics as in the body of the handwriting sample. In such a case, you can usually conclude that the writer is at peace with himself, does not want to appear what he is not, does not want to be conspicuous, and is sincere and stable. Before completing your analysis, however, you must examine the handwriting itself, to see whether these properties correspond to the features in the handwriting.

Additions – at times you will find a signature which is composed only of additions, i.e., something which initially was a signature, or some letters from the full name, and which became a scribble in the course of time. The simplest addition to a signature is a period. In most cases, the period appears at the end of the signature, and signifies its conclusion. The use of a period after the signature may suggest that the writer is subconsciously worried that something may be added to his signature, or that someone may try to forge it. This added point is a kind of protection for the signature itself.

You should examine the form of this period under a magnifying glass. You have to determine whether it is stable and static, or whether it resembles a comma; whether this represents an attempt to quench the writer's enthusiasm or a balanced, logical, pause. If the point closely resembles a comma, you can assume that it was produced at high speed (the greater the resemblance to a comma, the higher the speed). If it resembles a circle, this means that it was more thought-out, and has a different meaning. A static point is generally produced by slow writing, and indicates to you balanced judgment and a feeling of completion. It may also mean suspiciousness and an attempt to keep a safe distance. A light point, maintaining momentum, is made almost unconsciously, and is the result of speediness and the desire to stop at a certain point.

The difference between the signature and the text and the location of the signature are both important for your analysis.

While handwriting tells us about the writer's inner feelings, the signature tells us what the writer wants to be, what image he wants to convey. At times you can learn from the signature about the writer's past, his ambitions, and his expectations.

You must rely more on your intuition when analyzing signatures. There are several rules, but the general picture can be gained only intuitively.

Now let's look at the signatures of some famous people.

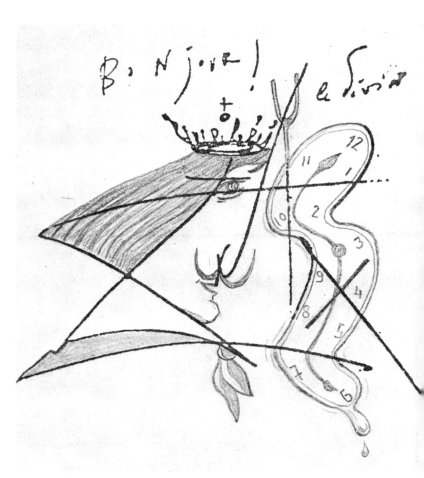

Salvadore Dali

This is the signature of Salvadore Dali, the famous surrealist artist. His extravagant signature spreads out over a full half page. You can see that the lines of his signature are very severe and stubborn.

Jayne Mansfield

This is Jayne Mansfield's signature. Like Dali's, it also is very big. But you can see that her signature is soft and round, with warmth replacing Dali's severity. Both Dali and Mansfield attempt to draw attention to themselves, but in different ways.

Steve McQueen

Telly Savalas

Steve McQueen, who's played a race driver on the screen, has a signature resembling an automobile.

Telly Savalas includes his trademark, his bald head, in his signature.

Walt Disney

Tom Wilson

Look at the signature of Walt Disney, the man who made Mickey Mouse and Donald Duck famous. Disney animates his letters. His signature exhibits much vitality, lightness, humor, and movement, just like his many cartoons.

It won't take much effort to see the similarities between Walt Disney's signature and that of the cartoonist Tom Wilson, the creator of "Ziggy."

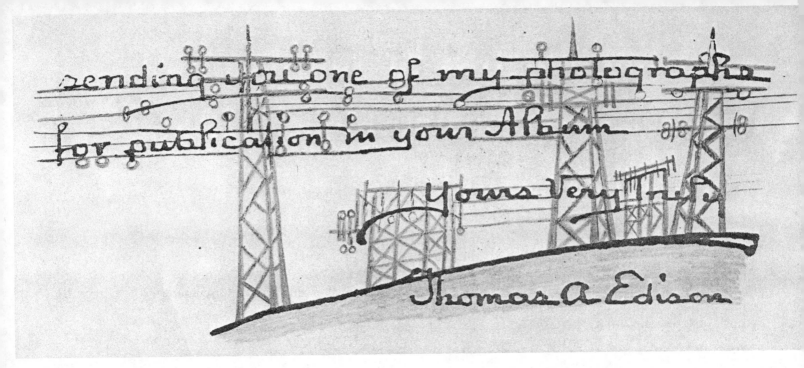

Now look at the signature of another famous person, in a completely different field of endeavor: Thomas Alva Edison, the famous inventor responsible for the electric light, phonographs, and many other technological breakthroughs that we take for granted today. What do you see here? A blueprint, or a large structure.

Thomas Alva Edison

This signature is that of David Ben–Gurion, Israel's first Prime Minister. His signature exhibits a great deal of power, momentum, self-confidence, and decisiveness.

David Ben–Gurion

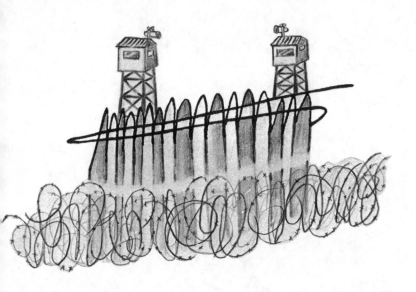

Paul

Paul's signature, which looks like a barbed wire fence, consists of 17 loops (never 16 or 18) crossed by two quick strokes. I learned why Paul's signature resembles a fence: he is a concentration camp survivor. Despite his attempts to wipe out the past, he cannot free himself of the burden of his memories and is still haunted by the camp fence. He was about 17 years old during the Holocaust; his signature is a concrete reminder of his past.

Our next signature is that of a cardiologist. If you look closely, you can see the resemblance between the signature and an electrocardiogram.

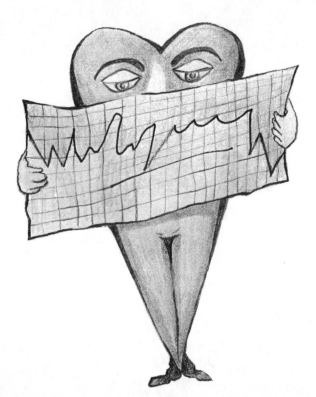

Cardiologist

Even though this signature is written in Hebrew, you can see that it looks like three medallions. This should tell you of the need to be important, and the desire to be worshipped by others. And what does he give in return? Three inflated balloons!

Here are another two inflated signatures, by people who want the admiration of others. The first person, however, has much more to offer than the second one.

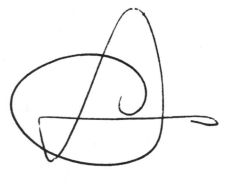

It doesn't take too much imagination to see Elvis Presley's guitar in the signature of the late rock 'n' roll star.

You can easily see the stage in the signature of Mercedes Sosa, the singer.

The signatures of a famous actor and actress, Peter Strauss and Liz Taylor, display no modesty. On the contrary, their signatures reflect their overwhelming desire to be seen and to perform, a desire which drove them to their current superstar status.

Yehudit, on the other hand, writes her name and then immediately surrounds it with a completely closed frame, which reveals her isolation and difficulties in making contact with other people.

Elvis Presely

Mercedes Sosa

Peter Strauss

Liz Taylor

Yehudit

Ada

Our next signature suggests that its owner finds it difficult to communicate. His signature is very crowded and cramped, and ends with a line crossing the entire signature. After having drawn himself with so many lines, a bold stroke goes over the signature canceling out his creation, and himself in the process. The many lines point to a great deal of stubbornness, rigidity, and wickedness. The name itself is illegible, indicating to you that the author has no interest in being understood.

Ada's signature has a message transcending the Hebrew in which it was written. Ada suffers from hearing problems, and her signature is a drawing of an ear.

Our next signer draws a roof above his head (the upper part of his signature), and the lower part of the signature is also well-developed. I learned that he is building his own home, and spends every free minute on renovations and additions to the house. You can see that the importance of his house in his life is represented by this roof. The extremely prominent lower region points, as you know, to highly developed sexuality.

The writer of our next signature is highly attached to his work. He is a pilot, and his signature forms a drawing of an airplane.
David always dreamed of being a pilot, and becomes one in his signature.

David

a businessman

an accountant

a sculptor

This signature belongs to a businessman. Despite his writing "letters," you can't read a single letter in his signature. He apparently is hiding his real intentions, maintaining the same poker face he wears while conducting negotiations.

This signature reveals artistic talent (a profile), as well as an inclination to deal with numbers (you can see the number 9 in his signature). The owner of this signature is an accountant, who paints in his spare time.

Our next signature is that of a sculptor, who has drawn a self-portrait in his signature. The additions at the left are his mustache and beard.

The author of this signature is an astrologist. It's no coincidence that you can see the celestial bodies in his signature.

an astrologist

It's pretty obvious that this signature, reproduced in full size, was written by a person who seeks to be noticed.

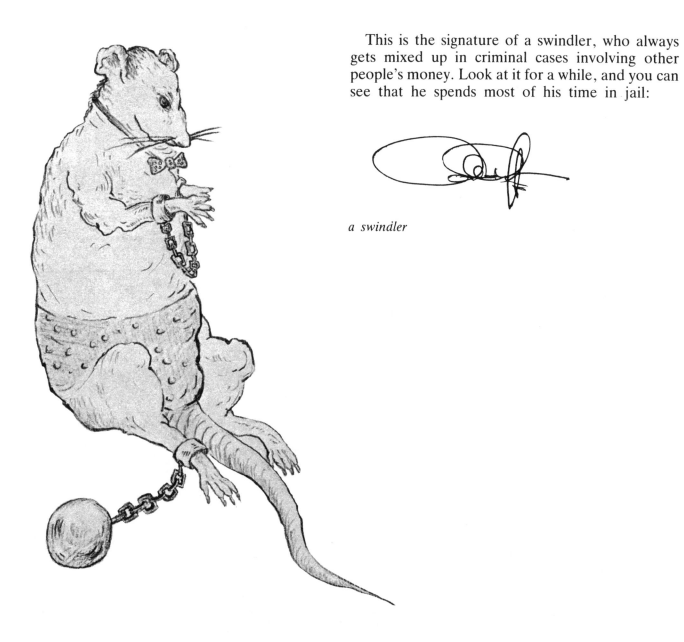

This is the signature of a swindler, who always gets mixed up in criminal cases involving other people's money. Look at it for a while, and you can see that he spends most of his time in jail:

a swindler

Now look at this signature of another prisoner,
reproduced full-size. The signature's thread shape
indicates adaptability – the flexibility of a snake.

Robin Fishell

On a lighter note, look at Robin Fishell's signature – his namesake, a fish, appears in his signature.

Position of Signature on Page

Graphological features	Character features
very large space between text and signature	*feeling of loneliness, distance, lack of contact with family or society*
very small space between text and signature	*dependence on family or society*
one line between text and signature	*recognition of value of society and of his need to belong to society and his family; need for society; balanced adjustment; wants to be known as an individual within the group*
two lines between text and signature	*affiliation with society based on mutual advantage; considers it important not to lose his independence and individualistic personality*
at the end of the page, far from the text	*fears assimilation within society; keeps his distance, thereby maintaining his independence; pride, aloofness*
attached to final margin	*balanced, well adjusted, courageous*
in the middle of the page, close to the text	*security wall; afraid to assume responsibility; speaks in the plural ("we"); feels that he is part of the whole*
in the middle of the page, far from the text	*avoids any personal risk; afraid of failure; lacks courage*
at the left margin of the page	*introvert; prefers a "safe" life; avoids doubts or risks; proud*

Graphological features	Character features
signature same size as text	*positive mutual relationship between writer and his surroundings*
first letter of first name larger than first letter of last name	*sensitivity over his "reputation," need for admiration, haughtiness*
first name different and exaggerated, in comparison with last name	*narcissistic need for attention*
small initial letters	*lack of self-confidence, low self-esteem*
last name larger than first name	*family pride, importance of family and social status*
different slant in first and last names, or different pressure and speed, or mistakes and corrections in one of the names	*family conflict, bickering, argument; tension or perplexity concerning family issues*

And now for my final word. If you have read this entire book carefully and methodically, you will be able to form an opinion about any handwriting sample you come across. But I want to emphasize once again: you are not a graphologist, and you must be doubly careful of using your newly acquired knowledge, and the professional "secrets" I have revealed to you. You have to decide now whether graphology will remain just an interesting topic, or whether you will continue to study this fascinating field thoroughly.

BIBLIOGRAPHY

Roman Klara, Handwriting; pantheon, N.Y., 1952
Roman Klara, Encyclopedia of written word; Frederick Ungar Publishing Co. Inc.
Nadya Olyanova, Handwriting Tells; 1968, Peter Owen, London
Nadya Olyanova, The psychology of Handwriting, Melvin Rowers, 1969
Paula Friedenhain, Write and Reveal; Peter Owen, London, 1959
Jacoby. H.J., Self knowledge through handwriting; books for professionals
Klages Ludivig, Handschrift und Charakter;
Bovier Verlag, Herbert Grundmann, Bonn, 1974
Falcon Hal, Cornerstone Library, N.Y. 1974
Paterson Jane, Interperting Handwriting; Macmillan, London Limited, 1976
Hearns Rudolph, Handwriting: an analysis through its symbolism; Vantage Press Inc., 1973
Paul de Sainte Colombe, Grapho-Therapeutics; popular library N.Y. 1972
Singer Eric, A Manual of Graphology; Duckworth 1974
Singer Eric, Personality in Handwriting; Duckworth 1974
Dr. Richard Pokorny, Systematic Graphlogy; Massada Publishing Ltd, Israel 1970
Israel Odem, Character and Handwriting; Bialik Institute and Dvir Co. Israel 1960
Israel Odem; Handwriting and personality; Bialik Institute and Dvir Co. Israel 1977
Israel Odem,   Hakibutz Hameuchad, Israel 1981
Israel Odem, Handwriting and Reality; Dvir Co. Israel 1981
Klara Roman, Encyclopedia of the Written word; Frederich Ungar Publishing Co.; 1968